From Prime Time
to My Time

From Prime Time to My Time

Andrew Green

warc

First published 2010 by Warc Ltd
1 Ivory Square, Plantation Wharf, London SW11 3UE, United
Kingdom

www.warc.com

ISBN 978-1-84116-219-5

A CIP catalogue record for this book is available from the
British Library.

Typeset by HWA Text and Data Management, London
Printed and bound in Great Britain by the MPG Books Group

Contents

Acknowledgements

I would like to thank the following friends, colleagues and advisors who have read early drafts of different chapters and sent me their comments. These have made this a much better book than it would have otherwise been.

Marion Appel, Director, Media Research, Intomart GfK
David Brennan, Research & Strategy Director, Thinkbox
Neil Eddleston, Managing Director, J.C. Decaux OneWorld
Thomas C. Evans, Vice-President, Audio Research & Special Projects, ESPN
Roger Gane, Research Director, RSMB
Scott C. McDonald, Senior Vice-President of Research, Condé Nast Publications
Erhard Meier, Ipsos MediaCT
Katherine Page, Technical Advisor, NRS Ltd
Irena Petric, Managing Director, Nationaal Onderzoek Multimedia
Richard Silman, CEO, Ipsos MediaCT
John Stockley, Senior Director, Ipsos MediaCT
Richard Windle, Chief Research Officer, Ipsos MediaCT
Rachel Wright, Business Development Director, Phonevalley

I would also like to thank Richard Silman and Didier Truchot of Ipsos who have allowed me the time to pull this all together. Without them it would never have happened.

Andrew Green
Sampford Courtenay, Devon.
15 July 2009

Foreword

At Ipsos, we have examined and researched many of the issues faced by our media clients over the last 50 years. Change is now happening at a faster rate than at any time in my own 25 years in this business. One only needs to consider how rapidly a service like Twitter, which nobody had heard of three years ago, has built a user base of many millions in such a short time to appreciate the scope and pace of such change.

Developments are occurring across platforms, content and business models and it is in the light of this that Ipsos developed its MediaCT specialism to help clients deal with the myriad of inter-media and intra-media business issues.

I have known Andrew for over 20 years. In all of that time I have been a supplier of media research whilst for much of it Andrew has been a media research consumer. In that role he has used all types of media research (the good and the not so good!); across all types of media and, critically, in nearly all of the major media markets of today. This wealth of experience places him in an almost unique position to discuss the changes that have gone before, are happening now and are yet to come.

We hope that you will find this book informative, illuminating and interesting. We also hope that it will not only build your understanding of what has happened in the past (and why) but will also feed your knowledge of what is happening today and, more importantly, help you to be prepared for tomorrow.

Richard Silman
Chief Executive Officer, Ipsos MediaCT
July 2009

1   Introduction

Media research is not designed to find out the truth. It is a treaty between interested parties.
Rodney Harris, Media director of UK agency DMB&B in the 1980s

How many people watched the World Cup Final in 2006?

How do we know how many people watch a television programme or read a newspaper? Sometimes we read about it or hear about it in the media. It was announced in 2006, for example, that a billion people watched the World Cup Final of that year. More recently we were told that no fewer than *two* billion people watched the opening ceremony of the Beijing Olympic Games.

How do they know? Did they know whether or not *you* were watching or, if you did, how many people were with you at the time? Is there some kind of device which you don't know about attached to the back of your television set which tells the broadcaster whenever you are watching their programmes?

In most cases the answer is definitely not. Nobody really knows how many people tuned into the Beijing Olympic Games and they certainly don't know (unless you are part of a panel set up specifically for the purpose of measuring television viewing) what you, personally, watch on any given day.

But research companies can *estimate* how many people watched the Olympics. They do this through monitoring the viewing behaviour of panels of people specially set up to represent the viewing populations of every major country in the world. Regular tracking of television viewing takes place in one form or another in about 75 countries worldwide, much of it employing advanced technology which automatically detects (for panel members only) when a television is on and to which channel it is tuned.

Other methods are used to discover how many people are in a room when the set is switched on. The viewing records of these panels are then projected to the entire population and can be aggregated globally in order to calculate how many people, by country, watched a given programme.

In reality, few media commentators go to the trouble of carrying out such an elaborate exercise. As a result, many of the statistics quoted about numbers of television viewers to major events are not entirely accurate. But few people bother to check the figures.

In the case of the World Cup in 2006 however, somebody did. Initiative Media Futures, a specialist media research agency, collated individual audience estimates from each of 54 markets representing the greater part of the world's potential television audience.

They found that, rather than the one billion viewers originally claimed, the true figure was closer to 254 million.[1]

In the case of the audience claimed for the Olympic Opening Ceremony, this was estimated by Nielsen on the basis of actual viewing data in 38 countries. China represented almost half the total audience.

Does it matter?

Accurate statistics – or at least credible estimates – of the audience size to major television events like the World Cup or the Olympics may not matter to everybody, but they are vitally important to some.

The figures are important to the companies that sponsor these big events, like Coca-Cola and Sony, who spend millions of dollars to get their brands in front of these viewers and, understandably, would like to know how many people they are 'buying' face time with.

They are also important to the organisers of the events, who can use the audience statistics to estimate the value of the broadcasting rights – and the price they can charge when they sell those rights around the world.

Exactly the same is true at the individual country level. If a broadcaster wants to sell commercial advertising slots, they will need to be able to price them – which they do largely on the basis of the number and kinds of people expected to watch them.

The advertiser, too, will want to select slots that are likely to be seen by the people they are trying to sell their brand to. And they will pay a higher price if they expect there to be more of these people watching.

Audience information also matters for the people who make and schedule programmes. There are many questions they may seek answers to from audience data:

- When is the best time to schedule the evening news?
- Which kind of film will appeal to a Sunday-afternoon audience?
- What sorts of programme appeal to younger men?
- Is viewing to a new series going up or down?

Other media

What is true of television is no less true of other media. The media are like any other consumer product: they need to understand their customers and their markets.

For newspapers and magazines, for example, customers are both readers and advertisers. So publishers need to understand their readers: How many are there? What kinds of people are they? Which competitive publications are they also reading?

Radio stations have the same requirements vis-à-vis their listeners, whilst website providers need to understand the internet audience. Newer purveyors of content like mobile phone companies are also beginning to dabble in the audience research arena.

It's not as easy as it sounds

Counting the numbers of people who watch, read, listen to, browse or search for content of all kinds is now a vast industry, drawing on both the skills of the market researcher and, increasingly, of advanced technology.

As will be argued in this book, research methodology is very important, even if many eyes glaze over at the thought of it. Seemingly arcane decisions such as how exactly a 'viewer', a 'listener' or a 'reader' are defined can make a major difference to the numbers reported in the estimates.

To go back to the example of the opening ceremony of the Beijing Olympic Games, should we measure the number of viewers who watched the whole 4-hour spectacle, or is it sufficient to count everybody who watched any part of it? The number will be very different.

For a newspaper, do we only consider readers who look at every page or do we also include those who may have simply glanced at a few articles – or even just the front page as they browse at a newsstand? Again, the answers will be different.

On the internet, is the number of machines that open a website page the same as counting the number of people who look at it?

And can we simply count the traffic walking or driving by a poster site and call that the 'audience'?

Hundreds, if not thousands of academic papers have been published on the rather obscure subject of how readership should be measured.

Questions such as how you measure hundreds of different magazines on a single survey can be tackled in different ways (as we shall see). The order in which you ask about publications in an interview can affect readership claims, as can the way in which you show them to respondents.

In fact there are almost as many ways to measure audiences as there are surveys. Every approach is slightly different – the result of history, the specifics of a marketplace or the way a survey is funded.

Global advertisers periodically call for methodologies to be 'harmonised' across markets so they can make valid comparisons of what they are getting for their money across countries. They would like to know that when they spend $100,000 to reach a million viewers, the term 'viewers' refers to the same thing whether you count them in Germany, Greece or Guatemala.

Unfortunately they are not. A 'viewer' in some countries is simply somebody who watches a programme where the advertiser's commercial runs. In others, it is the average number of people watching the commercial break – which may contain several other advertisements. Yet in some, the measurement will cover the number of people estimated to be in front of the screen at the precise time an individual commercial aired.

It has been difficult to get agreement on how these approaches can be harmonised. The major reason for this is that the companies contributing the bulk of funding to television audience measurement are the television stations – which are generally local companies with limited interest in what goes on outside their markets and plenty of interest in being able to compare their audiences over time.

Advertisers contribute very little directly to the funding of audience measurement services – though they are keen to point out that, in the end, it is their money that is being used and it is largely for their benefit that audiences are being measured in the first place. But it remains the case that it is the television stations that call the shots.

A business like any other

Because yes, audience measurement is a business just like any other, with profit and loss at the heart of it. So the cost of measurement has to be weighed against the value of the service provided.

Nobody could afford a perfect measurement – equipping every household in the country with a meter to monitor their television usage and every person with a device that records what they watch, listen to, click on or read although, with the exception of the reading part, it would be technically possible.

For a start, most people would not participate. The majority of people in most countries either refuse to take part in market research surveys or cannot be contacted. With the massive onslaught of direct marketing by email, letter and phone, many have become wary of responding to requests from strangers to take part in interviews.

Some have created barriers that automatically keep survey companies at bay: they may live in gated communities or doorman-controlled buildings – or simply refuse to answer the door to strangers.

The telephone can be just as problematic. Answerphones are used to screen calls and a growing proportion of homes no longer even have landlines, preferring to rely on their mobile phones – creating complications for market research companies trying to randomly dial a sample of the population.

And while on-line research has been the major beneficiary of these developments – getting on for half of all the market research interviews carried out in some countries – this method cannot reach everybody either.

So a census of audience measurement is impractical and would, in any case, be financially out of reach for anybody but the government (and even governments baulk at carrying out a census more frequently than once every ten years or so, given the costs and logistics of such exercises).

So samples are drawn to represent the populations being surveyed, with great care taken to minimise any kind of bias amongst the people chosen to take part (it would, for example, be inaccurate to recruit only the heaviest internet users or television viewers to represent the broader population's surfing or viewing habits).

These samples are then surveyed or otherwise tapped to provide the information needed about what they watch, listen to, read or browse.

The point about this is that pinpoint accuracy is neither sought nor achieved in these surveys. They are neither promising nor trying to obtain precise figures on the number of people watching a given television programme or reading a particular magazine. The cost of achieving this, as noted above, would be prohibitive.

What they are trying to do is to obtain a set of audience estimates that all users of the data feel is a reasonable approximation of the truth. That means that the information should be consistent over time (audience figures should not fluctuate unreasonably), they should make sense (newspapers and magazines know how many copies they sell; television stations know which programmes are being talked about) and the research should be credible (carried out to accepted quality standards).

This book is about how audience measurement has evolved over the last 80 years or so to meet the challenges of the twenty-first century. And it also offers a glimpse into the future, now that the world has gone inexorably on-line and mobile.

The ARF's eight steps

The Advertising Research Foundation (ARF) in the United States has usefully classified the measurement of media performance for advertisers into a hierarchy of eight different levels,[2] as follows:

1   *Vehicle distribution.* This is the foundation for any audience measurement system. It is a count of the number of physical units on which a piece of content (programming or advertising for instance) appears. Examples include the number of page views obtained by a website, the number of television sets switched on or the number of copies of a magazine or newspaper sold or distributed.

    Internet page views are automatically measured, as they are essentially an electronic request to a website for it to load a web page. The circulations of newspapers and magazines are independently audited in many countries, giving a fairly accurate picture of the numbers of copies being sold or distributed (minus the copies returned to the publisher).

Television tuning cannot be measured directly (except in homes receiving their signals via advanced cable systems), but is a by-product of electronic audience measurement systems. Out of Home media such as posters are often less organised than other media. But in some countries a lot of effort has gone into listing, mapping and even attaching GPS coordinates to each site location.

We will touch on these measurements.

2 *Vehicle exposure.* The next step up the hierarchy of audience measurement (and the main focus of this book) is a count of the number and types of people potentially exposed to the media being distributed.

It is obviously possible for more than one person to read a copy of a magazine or newspaper, even though only one person will have purchased it. Equally, one television can be watched by several people and a web page can be viewed by many people or by one person several times.

Surveys and a number of technologies are used to make these estimates, which are described more fully in the pages that follow.

An obvious problem with much of the research is the extent to which it can really tell us whether or not people are exposed to a vehicle. Poster audience measurement can provide estimates of how many people pass a site. But it cannot say if their heads were turned towards it. Television audience research generates estimates of how many people are in present in a room with a set switched on or who say they are 'watching' a given programme – but it cannot really tell us which of them are genuinely attentive to the screen at any point in time.

3 *Advertising exposure.* Advertisers are interested in going beyond vehicle exposure. Ideally, they want an estimate of how many and what types of people see or hear their particular message.

For television or radio, this means counting the people watching or hearing a commercial, not the programme or break it is appearing in. For print, it means measuring who reads particular pages or specific issues of a publication.

These data are available to varying degrees and to varying standards and we will touch on this.

4 *Advertising attentiveness.* Many advertisers track whether people can recall the advertising being aired or shown in various media. Results will depend only partly on whether the media placement was effective. The quality and execution of the message and the length of time it has been running also play an important role in influencing whether or not people will remember it.

It is possible to measure audience 'engagement' to different media in a number of ways, giving clues to whether a given advertisement is more or less likely to be remembered. For example, advertising can appear in programmes with a similar sized audience – but to which attention levels can vary considerably.

Banner ads placed carefully on a well-designed web page are likely to attract more clicks than a less well-placed ad on a poorly designed site. But it nevertheless remains true that people's attentiveness to advertising will be as much about the content and execution of the advertising itself as it will be about their engagement with the surrounding media context. It will also depend heavily on their levels of interest in the product being advertised.

We will look at some of the work carried out into audience attention to and engagement with the media, but the question of advertising attentiveness generally demands a book all in itself.

5 *Advertising communication.* This is a measure of the information retained by a consumer following exposure to an advertising message. It can be measured via tracking studies which ask people which ads for (e.g.) cars they can remember having seen and what message they can recall.

Creative execution is again a key factor, as well as media placement. The creative format of an advertisement is known to have an effect. Thirty-second advertisements on radio or television, for example, will generally have a higher communication impact than a 15-second ad.

Similarly, certain ad positions work better than others – whether it is the part of a web page where a banner appears or whether a print ad appears early or late in an issue.

We will review some of the work in this area.

6 *Advertising persuasion.* The persuasiveness of an ad can be gauged through methods such as copy testing (examining whether a proposed advertisement in any medium has the desired effect on

a sample audience before running it) or by asking people over a period of time about their intention to purchase brands (e.g. before and after advertising has aired). These techniques will not be covered in this book.

7 *Advertising response.* On the internet, it is possible to directly measure the number of visitors to a page or website who click on an ad or who subsequently take an action on-line (short of a purchase) in relation to any advertising they have been exposed to.

It has also long been possible to measure the number of people redeeming newspaper coupons, visiting car showrooms or calling toll-free numbers in response to advertising.

This measure is only available to companies who include some sort of feedback device in their advertising (such as a number to call or action to take). On the internet, of course, interactivity is built into the medium.

But even there, people may be exposed to ads on a web page and subsequently go on to purchase something off-line. This is not so easily measured.

Again, this subject is largely outside the scope of this book.

8 *Sales response.* The final link in the chain is the sale. On-line, it is possible to measure the number of people actually purchasing a product, although, as noted above, a limitation of this is that people may carry out a good deal of research on-line and then visit a store for their actual purchase, creating no link between their surfing behaviour and their actions.

An increasingly popular approach, especially for fast-moving consumer goods companies with rich data on sales and marketing, is to use econometric techniques to build models of how sales link to advertising.

The models examine the influence of important variables like price, distribution and seasonality, as well as marketing, in order to diagnose what the ideal mix of these elements should be. Amongst the marketing influences, they can examine such factors as the weight of advertising, the share of voice achieved in a market and the mix of different advertising media used.

Data on all these variables is collated and examined over a period of two or more years in order to establish what relationships – if any – have existed historically between them.

The creation of an econometric model has been likened to the baking of a cake. But in this case you start with the 'cake' (the sales performance of a brand) and knowledge of what most of the key ingredients are (price, media weight and mix, distribution etc).

The task is to work out in which quantities the ingredients were mixed to create the cake – and then to work out how you could bake an even better one.

Future challenges

After more than eighty years of gradually developing sample-based methods to measure media audiences, the signs are that the world is on the cusp of a major revolution in how people consume media. This will, in turn, have very substantial implications for the business and practice of audience measurement.

The digital revolution is transforming the way people consume news, entertainment and other content. Posters are popping up in the most unlikely places, some of them able to change copy at the touch of a button.

Newspaper and magazine content is available – usually for free – on-line and via mobile devices. Video can be streamed or downloaded to computers and mobile phones, where once it was only available via a television set.

Accompanying all this has been a massive explosion in the amount of content available to consumers via all these new distribution methods. Most people can receive many more television channels than they ever could before – often several hundred via cable or satellite services.

Radio stations broadcast globally over the internet and the internet itself now carries around 33 billion individual web pages of information – a number which rises by the day. With such a broad array of viewing, reading and listening options, it is becoming less and less likely that very large numbers of people will end up looking at the same content at the same time.

No economically feasible sample can possibly be expected to represent these many thousands of individual media options in a statistically reliable manner. For example, 470 channels were listed by the regulatory agency Ofcom as broadcasting in the UK at the end of 2007.

The organisation responsible for audience measurement (BARB – the Broadcasters' Audience Research Board) surveys 5,100 households on a continuous basis. Even with this size of sample they are unable to report on more than 250 channels due to the number of people in the sample being too low.

If just 1% of the households in the sample tune into a channel in a given week this will only amount to 51 of them. They will not all watch every programme – so most programmes will register no viewing at all.

Hence the title of this book. Historically, 'prime time' is defined as the time of day when most people are watching television or listening to the radio.

Fifty years ago, when the number of television and radio stations amounted to just a handful and the internet was merely a glimmer in J.C.R. Licklidler's eye, people watched the same programmes, listened to the same radio stations and read the same magazines and newspapers – often at the same times. The mass media was in the ascendant and audience measurement was relatively straightforward. People were also friendlier to interviewers and happier to take part in surveys.

Today, the growth in media options has meant that people can construct their own broadcast schedules using the internet, digital video recorders or other technologies. They can update themselves on the news or sports results whenever they want to using the internet or a mobile device.

They are no longer at the mercy of broadcast schedulers or newspaper editors. They can seek out and consume the content they want, when they want it.

There are still 'events' (such as the Olympic Games referred to earlier) which bring people together to watch the same programmes at the same times. But it is rare to see half of the population watching the same television show or listening to the same radio station on the same evening any more.

New approaches are being devised to measure and track these fragmenting and segmenting audiences. Instead of measuring prime time, we now have to measure 'my time'. Sample-based surveys will play a part in this, but they cannot provide the only answer.

Big Brother

Which brings us neatly back to a sentence which featured earlier in this chapter. It asked, you may recall, whether there was 'some kind of device which you don't know about attached to the back of your television set which tells the broadcaster whenever you are watching their programmes?'

It went on to say that 'in most cases the answer is definitely not'. But those who receive their television service from an advanced cable network operator like Charter Communications in Los Angeles or BSkyB in the UK may have been asked by their service provider whether they would agree to have their television viewing monitored – automatically – in the interests of research.

A company called Canoe Ventures in the United States, owned by the six major cable networks, is in discussion (at the time of writing at the end of June 2009) with various parties as to how it can harness the power of the 60 million cable set-top boxes operated by its owners for advertising purposes.

These set-top boxes, which sit behind viewers' televisions, can be programmed to track what happens every time the set is switched on – which channels are viewed, how long they are viewed for, when the channels are changed – every second.

Although it has not yet been widely adopted as a measurement methodology, the technology is now available for sets to be monitored like this – as long as people give the service providers permission to do so. So in these cases the users are asked. But will this be true everywhere in the world?

For newer media like the internet and mobile phones, tracking the behaviour of users is in-built. Internet Service Providers and Mobile Service Providers know every detail of their users' behaviour as and when it happens – as long as they are connected to the internet or mobile phone network. Even the poster industry is now incorporating automatic traffic counts made on behalf of traffic planning authorities into their measurement.

Technology for monitoring people's behaviour is moving faster than the regulators, who have often raised concerns about consumer privacy and whether in fact the capture and sale of what is claimed to be 'anonymised' data on people is in fact as anonymous as is claimed.

Researchers from the University of Texas, for example, recently developed a 'de-anonymisation algorithm' which allowed them to identify the real identities of around one third of apparently anonymous users of

Twitter, a popular social network, through analysing people's networks of connections.[3]

Radio Frequency Identification (RFID) chips are tiny tags used by manufacturers to track inventory as it moves from factory to warehouse to store. Attempts have been made to attach these tags to magazines with the aim of tracking which pages people look at. Only limited progress has been made with this technology at the time of writing; however this too may be of interest to audience researchers in the future.

In short, audience measurement is pursuing several leads in its pursuit of truth and accuracy: one involves technologies that provide detailed and passive measurement of the *devices* people use to access content: televisions, computers, mobile phones – even cars (where they drive by a poster site). This is sometimes called 'site-centric' measurement.

Another is focused on the people themselves and what they claim to be doing or can be observed as doing. This is called 'user-centric' measurement and embraces survey-based research of the sort already described. Within this definition are a range of new approaches such as facial recognition (used to automatically identify individuals) and eye-tracking (recording what people look at), as well as improved versions of the meters carried by people and used to register their viewing, listening, browsing or travel behaviour.

A third is what are sometimes called 'hybrid' approaches which combine both of the above using various modelling and other data-integration approaches. In the end, as we shall argue in this book, it is the hybrid approach which is likely to win through.

Organisation of this book

In summary, our intention is to review media audience measurement in all its major forms and to highlight some of the key studies carried out over the years, mainly in the English-speaking world.

We will occasionally use the words, 'audience measurement "currency"' in the text – this is employed by advertising and media practitioners to refer to the use of audience numbers as a form of trading currency; the audience figures are accepted by both buyers and sellers of media space as a measure of value applied to television commercials, radio advertising and newspaper and magazine space.

Two other terms are worth clarifying at the outset:

- *Audience ratings*: this is an expression of audiences in percentage terms. If there are 100,000 adults in a population and 50,000 of them watch a particular programme, this can be expressed as 50% of the population – or 50 ratings. If the *same* 50% watch a second programme, the two programmes together are said to have generated 100 ratings. In other words, people are counted every time they watch (or listen, or read) – and totals can exceed 100%.
- *Audience reach*: in the example above, the audience reach would be 50%. However many different programmes this same 50% watch, there are still 50% who did not watch – so the reach can never exceed 100% and nobody is counted more than once.

The rest of the book will look in detail at audience measurement for each of four 'traditional' media – print, Out of Home, radio and television. We then turn to two newer media: the internet and mobile, concluding with an overview of multi-media audience measurement. Each of these media will be examined under five broad headings:

1   An historical overview of the medium;
2   The origins and development of audience measurement;
3   How audience size and composition is estimated today;
4   Measures of attention and engagement; and
5   Future challenges.

I hope you find it useful and informative.

2 Measuring print media audiences

> We do not talk – we bludgeon one another with facts and theories
> gleaned from cursory readings of newspapers, magazines and digests.
>
> Henry Miller

Origins of print media

Like the compass, gunpowder, bells, wooden coffins, bank notes, dominoes, fireworks, cameras and toilet paper, printed media can be said to have been invented in China. It was there, approximately 5,000 years ago, that the first forms of writing ink were developed for blackening stone-carved images. The ink was made from mixing lampblack or soot with glue made out of animal hides and bone black pigment. The substance was moulded into sticks, dried and mixed with water before use.

It was again in China that the earliest known form of paper had its origins. The ancient Egyptians had been using beaten strips of papyrus plants to write on since at least 3500 BC – hence the word 'paper' – but it was the Chinese who introduced paper in its modern form.

Until at least the birth of Christ, documents in China were generally written on bamboo, bone or silk. These were either too difficult to transport or – in the case of silk – too expensive to produce in any quantity.

Tsai Lun, an official attached to the Imperial Han court, has been credited with the invention of this new form of writing material, for which he was handsomely rewarded (there is some historical controversy over whether in fact paper was already being used by the Chinese military 100 years earlier).

Although the exact formula has been lost, it is known that he mixed ingredients like the bark of mulberry trees, hemp, silk rags and fishing nets to create the paper.

In 593 AD, the earliest form of woodblock printing on paper was pioneered – again in China. In this process, text was written in ink onto a sheet of paper. The written side was then placed onto a smooth block of wood coated with rice paste. The un-inked parts of the rice paste were then carefully cut away leaving the reversed text in relief to dry.

Moveable type printing was pioneered by a Chinese alchemist, Pi Sheng, in the eleventh century using a mixture of glue and clay to manufacture the characters. Texts were composed by placing the types onto an iron plate coated with resin, wax and paper ash. The plate was heated, then cooled, solidifying the type. It could then be detached and re-used simply by heating the plate again.

Early newspapers

With ink, paper and printing, the technical underpinnings for a written mass media were in place by the end of the sixth century. But the practice of collecting and disseminating information to a body of readers had already existed for several hundred years in China by this time with the *Di Bao* or palace reports. These imperial bulletins carried news from the emperor's court to a carefully selected audience of bureaucrats.

The best candidate for the accolade of being the world's first newspaper, however, probably goes to the *Acta Diurna* (daily public records) of ancient Rome, which featured a range of content including the outcome of court trials, public notices and even, eventually, news of prominent births, marriages and deaths. *Acta Diurna* dated from 131 BC. In 59 BC, Julius Caesar made proceedings of the Senate public through these notices.

Before fast-forwarding to the invention of more advanced printing processes in fifteenth-century Europe, it is worth mentioning one other legacy China bequeathed to the modern media world: that of media censorship.

Censorship itself was neither new nor unique to China in the ninth century – the country's first censorship law had been introduced in 300 AD. But it was then that the emperor Wen-tsung (827–840 AD) issued a decree forbidding the private printing of almanacs by local governments.

Laws and regulations designed to protect the state's exclusive audiences in compiling and distributing certain printed materials continued to evolve during the Song Dynasty (906–1229 AD) with punishments as severe as 100 blows with a heavy stick for transgressors.

By 1160 the Song emperor had recognised the power of the press when he was petitioned to suppress a condensed version of the *Di Bao* (*Hsiau-Pao* or 'Little Press') popular with peasants for the crime of 'rumour-mongering'.[1]

Officially, the first 'proper' newspaper, *Relation aller Fürnemmen und gedenckwürdigen Historien* ('Collection of all distinguished and memorable news') started life in Germany in 1605[2] and was followed by the rapid development of the medium throughout the world over the next 300 years.

By 2008 more than 12,000 newspapers were being published with a reputed 539 million copies sold and 40 million given away every day.[3] From the slim, text-heavy, black-and-white issues of the nineteenth and early twentieth centuries, newspapers have introduced colour and photography, they have fattened up and sprouted multiple sections and supplements and, of course, they have gone on-line and mobile.

Content previously available according to the distributor's schedule, can now be uploaded continuously as it happens. Articles can be expanded, referenced and linked to other information. Thousands of newspapers from around the world can be accessed quickly and easily via the internet.

In short, newspapers are now just one way in which the content produced by journalists, writers and photographers can be accessed.

Magazines

Germany was also the home of the world's first magazine, *Erbauliche Monaths-Unterredungen* ('Edifying Monthly Discussions'), which was issued periodically from 1663.

The usage of the word 'magazine' is thought to have originated with the launch in 1731 of the *Gentleman's Magazine* by Edward Cave, which included Samuel Johnson amongst its contributors. Others followed, covering a wide range of topics from fashion and leisure through to political and religious affairs.

By the end of 2008, the United States boasted 20,590 magazine titles,[4] compared with about 600 in 1950. There is a magazine for almost every conceivable interest, hobby and subject.

With a similar story in many other countries, magazines have been a success story for many years – although many are now challenged by the growing influence of the web (see below).

Audience measurement

Newspapers were the world's first mass medium. They were also the first to offer advertisers information on how many people were reading them – although in its early years this information was incomplete.

Two primary measures were, and are, used for both newspapers and magazines: circulation is a count of the number of copies sold or distributed; readership is estimated using surveys, which seek to establish how many and what kinds of people have been exposed to a given title (whether or not they have bought it themselves).

In order to calculate the readership of a publication, people can be asked either about their reading of *specific* issues of a given title (e.g. the May edition of a monthly magazine) or about their reading of *any* issue of a title within a given time period (such as the past month).

To ask about specific issues, as was the case in the United States for many years (using what was known as the 'Thru-The-Book' technique), an interviewer would physically carry copies (or at least stripped-down versions of them) of all the titles included in the survey to an interview.

They then took respondents through each title to which they had established a general readership claim in order to establish whether they had read that particular edition.

Quite apart from the logistical difficulties involved in this, many felt that such an approach underestimated readership insofar as readers may see an issue of, say, a monthly magazine, long after its cover date and so not be counted. But the main limitation was in the number of titles that could be included on a survey.

The approach adopted on most readership surveys simply asks people to state whether or not they have read or looked at any copy, of whatever age, of a given title in its publication interval – e.g. yesterday for a daily newspaper, in the past week for a weekly magazine and so on. The technique is known as 'Recent Reading'. It does not require interviewers to show actual issues of publications to respondents.

It is argued by proponents of the method that Recent Reading more effectively captures audiences for weekly and monthly magazines than the Thru-The-Book technique. A good example of why they believe this is due to extensive reading of old issues occurring in public places like doctors' waiting rooms – reading that is captured using the Recent Reading approach but not by Thru The Book.

Daily newspaper reading is not thought to be much affected by the technique used, as few people will bother to read very old newspapers. But it is a different story for magazines.

There have been fierce methodological debates over whether the Recent Reading technique is in fact biased in favour of monthly and longer-frequency titles.[5] In fact there have been – and continue to be – debates over every aspect of the readership measurement methodology.[6]

Such debates are a common theme in the history of all media audience measurement: media with poor results in a given survey will automatically assume that the methodology must be biased against them in some way. They are usually less vocal when results are good.

In the case of Recent Reading, one of the key battles was fought over two biases in the methodology known as 'replicated' and 'parallel' reading. The first refers to reading of a title over a longer period of time than its publication interval (e.g. taking more than a month to finish reading a copy of a monthly magazine).

For those who do not habitually read every issue of a monthly magazine, this means that a readership claim will be made outside the month in which the title appears, effectively *overstating* the probability of reading it.

On the other hand, parallel reading has the opposite effect: this occurs when somebody reads two separate issues of a magazine within one publication period and their probability of reading any given issue is then *understated* because they can only be counted once.

To the extent that one of these effects is greater than the other for one or more publication types, the Recent Reading model can be said to be biased.

With one or two minor exceptions, however, it is the Recent Reading methodology that has been adopted in most of the countries where readership surveys are carried out.

At the last count, there were at least 95 major readership surveys operating in 72 countries as well as countless other surveys of more specialist titles such as those targeting doctors, businessmen or IT professionals.[7]

Broadly speaking, the Recent Reading interview proceeds as follows:

1   Respondents are asked to look through a long list of newspapers and magazines in order to 'screen in' those they have read in the past 6–12 months (different surveys use different screen-in periods). These are usually presented in the form of cards or groups of similar titles, using logos or typescript to represent each publication.
2   Having screened out most of the long list, interviewees are then asked questions about the short list of titles that remain. Ideally, the titles are rotated in some way to minimise any 'order bias'.
3   They are quizzed about both the number of times they have read each title (e.g. how many of the past four issues) and about whether they have read it recently – i.e. yesterday for dailies, in the past week for weeklies or in the past 4 weeks for monthlies. This last question is the basis for calculating readership of an average issue.

It may be useful to look back at some of the earliest readership surveys in the United Kingdom and United States, where much of the early history of print measurement took place. Although they ended up using similar methodologies, the paths they followed to get there were very different.

The Audit Bureau of Circulations was created in the United States in 1914 to provide independent verification of the circulation claims of subscribing publications – in some ways the first print audience measurement body. Organisations with the same name and purpose were founded in the UK in 1931 and in Australia the following year. Such bodies are now fairly widespread – though by no means universal – around the world.

The UK: Print measurement (1928–2008)

In the United Kingdom, most of the earliest 'readership' surveys carried out were concerned not with readership as it is now understood but with circulation.[8]

Membership of the Audit Bureau of Circulation was not widespread in its early days, casting some doubt on the circulation claims made by publishers. The infant discipline of market research was instead brought in to produce more objective circulation estimates. The primary measurement unit was the household buying a publication rather than the individual reader.

Surveys sponsored by the advertising agency trade organisation, the Institute of Incorporated Practitioners in Advertising (IIPA) in 1930, 1931 and 1932 were all of this type. So was an even earlier study, *Press Circulations Analysed*, carried out by the London Press Bureau in 1928.

The surveys told us nothing about the age and sex of readers. Ad agency J. Walter Thompson addressed this by commissioning its own research into individual readers in 1933 – probably the first of its kind.[9]

In a subsequent survey carried out in 1938, JWT interviewed 17,000 people. As their promotional leaflet of the time boasted, their investigators 'stopped men in the street, talked to girls in factories (and) visited spinsters' whist-drives and bachelors' lodgings' in order to gauge their readership habits. Random probability sampling was still a few years away in this field.

In 1939, the *Survey of Press Readership*, sponsored again by the Institute of Incorporated Practitioners in Advertising, was launched – possibly the earliest 'proper' readership survey. 43,000 interviews were carried out with respondents selected by an elaborate quota system designed to be as representative as possible of every practicable combination of social class, age, sex and region.

The lower age-limit was 14 – the statutory school-leaving age in Britain at the time. The study covered 10 national daily newspapers, 12 national Sunday newspapers, 71 magazines and 101 regional morning and evening newspapers.

The technique used was the first known use of the Recent Reading approach. Respondents were asked about their reading of dailies on the previous day, of weeklies during the previous week and of monthlies during the previous month, on the assumption that the reading of any issue of a particular title during its latest 'frequency period' would represent the reading of an average issue during the whole of its life.

Visual prompts to memory were employed – in this case, lists of newspaper names and photocopies of the covers of the latest issues of each magazine. In addition, people were asked where they had obtained the title (e.g. bought a copy or read somebody else's) and whether or not the title was read 'regularly' (at least 4 issues a week of the daily newspapers, and at least every other issue of weekly and monthly publications).

Results were published only for the national dailies and Sundays and the four leading general weeklies.

As one of the pioneers in UK readership research wrote in 1990, many of the fundamentals of the survey have in fact changed little since:[10]

1   It covered in one questionnaire all the national newspapers and all the consumer magazines that were of any real significance for advertising purposes.
2   It measured the readership of individual 'adults' (most earlier work had used 'homes' as the reading unit).
3   It used what is now called 'recent reading' as the criterion of readership.
4   It measured 'regularity' of reading and source of copy.
5   It used visual aids to assist informants' memories.
6   It produced figures analysed by sex, class, age and region.
7   It produced duplication tables, and offered a procedure (albeit an imperfect one) for calculating, from these figures, the net coverage of multi-title schedules.

In 1947 several major readership surveys were undertaken. The IIPA published a follow-up survey to its 1939 effort. Hulton Press, publishers of a leading magazine of the day, *Picture Post*, also launched their own survey, the *Hulton Readership Survey* covering 87 publications of all types.

Both these studies used quota sampling and interviewed 12,000 people. Both, interestingly, also used the same research supplier, Research Services Limited (now part of the Ipsos Group).

Although readership results from the two studies were virtually identical, it was the Hulton Survey that was to dominate UK readership measurement until 1955. The reason was fairly straightforward: it was offered free of charge to any organisation which could claim a *bona fide* interest in advertising in the press.

Hulton also provided data on certain target groups so advertising agencies could analyse readership according to people's usage of a range of products and services. These included consumption of electricity or gas, actual and potential home ownership, possession of gardens and allotments, regular or occasional drinking of beer, wine and spirits, cigarette and pipe smoking, and more.

In marked contrast, the IIPA continued with its cloak and dagger approach: the results of both its 1939 and 1947 surveys were made available to subscribing advertising agencies only and on the strict condition that (to quote from the title page of the 1939 report): 'The contents of the Survey must in no circumstances be disclosed to a publisher.'

The other readership survey published in 1947 was the *Attwood National Publications Readership Survey*. It was based on a large (20,000) sample, though it covered only eight weekly magazines in addition to the national press, so was less comprehensive than that of its contemporaries. The Attwood study was available to anyone who paid a subscription to buy it.

By 1953, the Hulton Survey was coming in for increasing criticism as usage grew and advertising became more important for publishers. It was difficult for competitive publishers to accept that their fortunes rested on the honesty and accuracy of a commercial rival, however well the survey was run.

Associated Newspapers, a leading newspaper publisher, certainly felt aggrieved and decided to initiate – and fund – what was to become the third IIPA *National Readership Survey* (NRS) in 1954.

Amidst much recrimination and argument, it was 'adopted' by the IIPA before publication and thus bore the Institute's name (although, tellingly, the IIPA's official Research Committee neither knew about nor subsequently agreed to endorse the survey!).

Distribution was no longer restricted as previous IIPA surveys had been; the report was sold without restriction and could be quoted freely, subject only to acknowledgement of IIPA's copyright. However, many were unhappy with the results. Newspaper readership was up dramatically compared with Hulton's figures; magazine reading was significantly lower.

Many put this down to methodological flaws – such as asking respondents about their reading in a fixed order of titles, with daily newspapers asked about first and monthly magazines last. It was argued (and later proved) that publications asked about late in a long survey were disadvantaged. The Hulton Survey was still used by many agencies and publishers that year.

But there were no more Hulton Surveys after that, paving the way for the next stage in the UK's readership research history – the launch in April 1956 of the survey still in use today, the National Readership Survey.

It was mainly (around 80%) funded by publishers but run under the auspices of the advertising agencies. Fieldwork was continuous, with random probability sampling.

Publications were 'screened' to reduce the number asked about individually and the order in which they were asked was rotated to minimise bias.

A number of major changes were to occur to the survey over the next fifty years. Three years in particular have been singled out as 'landmark' years:[11]

1   **1968.** In 1968 there was one organisational and one technical development worth noting. In that year JICNARS (the Joint Industry Committee for National Readership Surveys) was formed, placing the survey under the joint control and management of the whole industry – as opposed to the agencies, which had been running it up until then.

   The technical development was the addition of a frequency question for each title on the survey ('how many out of x issues have you read'), followed by a question on how recently each title had been read or looked at. Though it may not seem revolutionary, it was through this change that it became possible to calculate readership probabilities and thereby to conduct schedule analysis.

2   **1984.** This was the year when the so-called Extended Media List method was introduced, increasing the number of titles measured on the NRS from 100 to 300 – without lengthening the interview. The old method had involved presenting titles one-by-one in a fixed order. The new method allowed titles to be grouped and rotated in various ways to minimise bias.

3   **1992.** In this year Computer Aided Personal Interviewing (CAPI) was introduced to the survey alongside a number of other technical improvements (i.e. the interviewer used a laptop computer to carry out the interview rather than the traditional clipboard and pen). This enabled a number of quality improvements to be made in the survey administration and data processing procedures.

In 2009, key challenges for the survey include dealing with falling response rates to personal interviews and coping with the growing influence of on-line readership of newspapers and magazines. But the method is still fundamentally the same as the one pioneered back in 1939 by the IIAP.

The United States: From Starch to MRI

In the United States at around the same time as the IIAP in Britain was publishing its third household circulation survey in 1932, Daniel Starch founded the *Starch Continuing Readership Research Program*. He had established his reputation analysing the readership of advertisements – known as the Starch Recognition Procedure.

He too focused on the household and the 'primary' reader or buyer of the magazine (newspapers were not a significant national medium in the United States). A national sample of households was contacted and asked which magazines they or their households subscribed to or bought at the newsstand.

Magazine logos (taking the place of advertisements in his standard surveys) were employed as recognition aids. Respondents were also asked whether they had read the most recently published (i.e. a specific) issue. Results were weighted (i.e. 'corrected') to reflect the circulation figures published by the Audit Bureau of Circulations.

Readership research proper started with *Life* magazine in 1938 after it was discovered that some issues were so popular they were selling out almost as soon as they hit the newsstands, causing people to beg, borrow or steal copies from the magazine's buyers. Circulation, it was clear, was not a true measure of the title's size or reach.[12]

They were less concerned than Starch was with whether people had purchased their copy – only that they had read or looked at it. In the earliest studies, quota samples of respondents were shown a full copy of the magazine which they were then taken through page by page and asked whether they remembered seeing it. Thru-The-Book was born.

As this proved cumbersome in several ways, the method was modified over the series of studies carried out from 1938 to 1947 known as *Life's Continuing Study of Magazine Audiences*. Eventually respondents were simply asked to look through the issue in question, focus on a few key editorial items and then to state whether or not they had seen that issue before.

Those who had were 'readers' – although it is worth pointing out here that *Life*'s publishers were keen to broaden the then-prevailing questions about 'reading' a magazine to take account of the fact they were primarily a publication of pictures. The question was tailored accordingly to 'read or seen this issue', one that is now standard in readership surveys around the world.

In 1947 Alfred Politz conducted his first print media audience study for Hearst's *Chicago Herald-American*. This was, it was claimed, 'the first media survey to use a real probability sample of individuals and to ask respondents also about yesterday's purchase of the media vehicle'.[13]

In 1950 Politz published his first survey for *Life* magazine, '*A Study of the Accumulative Audience of Life*'. This study also adopted the random probability sampling technique, replacing the previous quota sample. The survey went back to respondents two further times to establish the readership accumulation of the magazine – enabling advertisers and agencies to estimate how many people were likely to see their messages appearing in multiple issues of the magazine, as opposed to just a single edition.

In time, a few competitor titles were added to the *Life* survey, while other magazines conducted their own Politz surveys. The greatest weakness of the readership studies in the 1950s was that only a handful of titles could be measured on any one study, due to the difficulties of administering the Thru-The-Book interview. So most of them remained unmeasured. But for the next few years, Politz dominated the US magazine audience measurement field.

In 1962 Bill Simmons carried out his first study covering 36 magazines using the Thru-The-Book method to gauge average issue readership, employing stripped-down rather than complete issues as prompts. Total audience data was published (i.e. both the 'primary' and 'pass-along' readers were included) for a range of titles including mass circulation titles and more selective magazines for the first time in a single survey. He also collected information about other media and some limited marketing information. The study was expanded during the 1960s, adding more magazines, enhanced multiple-issue data and more product data via follow-up interviews.

In 1972, the Target Group Index (TGI) was launched using the British Recent Reading method. This allowed more magazines to be included.

The fact that it was administered as a self-completion questionnaire also allowed a lot more product information to be collected.

Readership estimates were much higher than the Simmons Thru-The-Book method had generated, an obvious attraction to many publishers, even if many research purists were concerned that the method inflated the audience estimates. Commercially, however, TGI was not a success and the survey was eventually merged with Simmons.

In 1979, MRI (Mediamark Research and Intelligence) entered the market using a new and improved Recent Reading method. By 'improved', the company meant that the readership questions were administered by personal interviews using visual prompts, while product data was collected in a leave-behind questionnaire.

By including more titles, charging lower prices and generating higher readership estimates than Simmons, it eventually prevailed as the 'currency' survey in the US market, but only after a decade of often acrimonious debate over the pros and cons of the two different approaches.[14]

Limitations of current readership measurement

Readership surveys, as described above, define audiences as 'Average Issue Readers', a broad measure which tells users of the data how many and what kinds of people read an average issue of a title on an average day – rather than a specific issue on a specific day.

Circulation data, equally, provides averaged data across multiple issues of a newspaper or magazine. This leads to one of the major limitations of print audience research: its lack of granularity.

Proprietary but unpublished research by several media agencies has often shown significant variation in newspaper readership from day to day. As a result, some countries have now begun to publish day-by-day readership estimates.[15] But they remain the exception rather than the norm.

Magazines, similarly, have varying circulation and readership levels from issue to issue, something of great interest to advertisers who must place their message in a specific, rather than an average issue.

In the United States, MRI began measuring the readership variation between specific issues of magazines at the end of May 2006 using a separate on-line study. These data are offered as a supplement (but not a replacement) to its main survey.[16]

Circulation vs. readership

One of the early findings from the MRI specific-issue data was that movements in circulation and readership from issue to issue did not always occur in the same direction. This is something that perennially confuses users of print audience research. Publishers in particular, who may be enjoying circulation growth, cannot believe it when readership levels do not rise as well (although they tend to be less quick to question readership numbers which fail to fall when circulation drops).

In fact, there is no reason at all why circulation and readership levels should rise and fall together. The rate at which people *buy* newspapers or magazines is not necessarily connected to the likelihood of people *reading* them – as magazines in particular tend to have several 'pass-along' readers, a number that can vary for completely different reasons.

There is nothing to prevent somebody who used to buy a magazine no longer doing so because they can now read somebody else's copy. Or they might start buying a magazine where they used to read somebody else's copy. Magnified on a large scale, such changes in individual behaviour can easily lead to trends in the two data series moving in opposite directions for a time.

Guy Consterdine noted at least twenty factors influencing the number of readers each magazine copy is likely to have in a study of UK magazine trends.[17] These ranged from the measuring instruments themselves (including changes in the readership methodology), demographics (e.g. the fall taking place in average household size across many developed countries affects whether people want or need their own copies of publications) and factors individual to magazines (e.g. the extent of public-place reading, the age of a title and competitive dynamics in the marketplace). Circulation was only one of these factors. He concluded that there simply wasn't a straightforward link between the two.

But this didn't stop people trying to uncover just such a link. An investigation into 148 US magazine titles over a five-year period, for example, found no statistical link between circulation and readership changes.[18] This was true of both established and new titles. Studies in Sweden and the UK have produced similar findings.[19]

When such comparisons are made, it is usually assumed that circulation numbers are the more robust number representing 'truth' while readership data are survey-based estimates and so subject to error. Any discrepancy between the two must lie in some kind of problem with the readership figures. But it is not as simple as that.

In the first place, the detail behind top-line circulation data – rarely seen outside the publishing houses – can be very significant in this respect. A study by researchers from Condé Nast in the United States looked at three-monthly upscale magazines over the period 1997–2002.

They found that the best correlation with readership estimates came not from total circulation, but from sub-sets of it: these included the number of single-copy sales, the percentage of sales going to public places and the percentage within that total distributed in beauty parlours.[20]

Such data demonstrate the perhaps obvious truth that different types of circulation generate different levels of readership. If the balance between the various types of circulation changes it will clearly have differential effects on readership estimates. Circulation is, of course, far more under the control of publishers than readership and can be manipulated to some extent for accounting or other reasons.

It is also possible for changes in circulation to *lag* changes in readership (rather than the other way around).[21] Examples like the magazine *Smash Hits* in the UK showed readership numbers rising before circulation followed – doubtless explained by target readers trialling other people's copies before buying their own. Another UK title *Miss* found that its readership declined before circulation began to fall and, later on, the same lagged effects showed themselves on the way back up.

Another reason circulation and readership may not move in step – and a second limitation of readership surveys – is the statistical variability of readership estimates.

Because readership numbers are derived from sample-based surveys, there will always be a degree of sampling variation in the results. For example, the main readership surveys in both the USA and the UK report readership within what are termed 95% 'confidence limits'.

This is a statistical way of saying that there is a high likelihood (not a certainty) that the actual readership of a publication will be within a specified range around the published estimate (e.g. the published number is not an exact figure, it is an *estimate*).

To take a hypothetical example, if a magazine is reported as reaching 16% of a target audience, it may technically mean (depending on the sample size and the penetration of the title amongst this audience) that there is a 95% likelihood that readership will fall within (say) the 14–18% range.[22]

In practice, most users of readership surveys do not concern themselves about details like this. However, it is important to know that when changes in readership occur within this range of error there has really been little or no change in the real number.

Where this happens, a relationship with circulation trends will be impossible to detect and probably accounts for many of the seemingly contradictory trends seen. This was the conclusion of a study of US magazine circulation and readership changes, which found 92% of all observations to have been within these statistical boundaries.[23]

There is, in short, no simple relationship between circulation and readership. So it is perfectly possible for readership to fall when circulation is rising (and vice versa).

A third limitation of industry surveys is that they can only ever capture data on the very largest publications (usually between 100 and 300 titles). Almost all the surveys are conducted face-to-face, which limits how many titles can be asked about. Most smaller titles will not register on such a survey unless the sample sizes are very large (which is likely to be prohibitively expensive).

Readership accumulation

A fourth limitation arises from the time it takes a publication to reach all its readers. When an ad appears on television, on the radio, as an internet pop-up or even in a daily newspaper, chances are that people will have an opportunity to be exposed to it on the day it airs or appears.

As Personal Video Recorders, podcasting and video-streaming services on the internet gain in popularity, this connection between the time of broadcast and when a programme is watched or listened to may become weaker. But in the short-term it is unlikely to approach the time horizons faced by monthly or bi-monthly magazines.

These can linger in people's homes, in doctors' waiting rooms or be passed around from person to person for many months after their official cover date has passed. An ad placed in a January issue, in other words, is unlikely to reach all its intended audience or to exert its full effect in that month.

Studies carried out around the world since the 1960s have concluded that monthly magazines in particular can take 12 or more weeks to reach their ultimate readership levels (as recorded in industry surveys) while weeklies could easily take three weeks to reach their full potential.[24]

Some of these studies used in-home interviews looking at specific issues of magazines to gauge how long after publication they were still being read. Others employed a diary approach where people were asked to keep a record of all the specific issues of publications they read (the first time they read them) over a period of time.

In the UK in 1990, Millward Brown[25] carried out some research into the readership lag phenomenon by interviewing 1,883 adult women face-to-face about their magazine reading. This was followed up by interviews with a similar number of men in 1991.

The interviews took the form of a 'pantry check' – collecting up any magazines lying around the house that had been read in the past fortnight – alongside questions about reading in the past week both of these and of any titles they did not still have in their possession. All reading of any issue was captured and recorded.

This enabled a picture to be built of how long specific issues were being read for. Millward Brown found that it could take as much as five months for 90% of a monthly magazine's total readership to build, with less than half occurring in the 4 weeks following its issue date.

A Belgian study[26] in 1998 interviewed 2,528 people over the course of three months, asking them about readership of the six most recent issues of titles they claimed to have read. Results indicated that official readership levels for weeklies tended to be reached after about two weeks whereas monthlies would take about 12 weeks.

In the United States, MRI adopted a diary-based approach[27] arguing that following the same group of people over a period of time had a number of advantages over interviewing different people at single points in time.

An important finding from this study was that the rate at which a magazine built its coverage over time was not simply dependent on its publication frequency; factors like the number of readers looking at each title, the content of the magazine and where it was read all had an impact.

Individual monthly publications varied in the rate they built coverage, but tended to reach 80–90% of their total readers within 12 weeks.

This can be a problem if a marketer is trying to model the impact of his magazine advertising against sales. This is now common practice amongst companies keen to measure the payback from all their major investments, including advertising.

In simple terms, a statistical model is built which tries to create a numerical database of all the possible influences on a brand's sales over time (e.g. price, distribution, seasonal factors, competitive activity and advertising weight). Variations in these influences are then compared with changes in sales to establish connections between the two sets of data.

It is relatively simple to feed such models with detailed television schedules and associated audiences for each commercial. But it is less straightforward for magazine advertising.

One possibility is that the model builder, with nothing to go on apart from the standard readership information, will make the false assumption that all readership falls into the month of issue. If it then emerges that the model shows very little sales impact occurring in that month, erroneous conclusions may be drawn as to the medium's effectiveness – although in reality less than half the recorded total readership of most monthly magazines may have been accumulated in the first month of issue.

Further studies into audience accumulation have been carried out in both the UK and the USA and linked to the official readership survey data, allowing media planners, should they so choose, to incorporate the time dimension into their schedules.[28]

A fifth limitation of standard print audience surveys is that they do not generally provide a measure of who sees individual advertisements or pages. They are designed as a measure of any reading of a publication, not to specific parts of it.

Advertisers, of course, place their messages on specific pages of specific issues, not on average pages in average issues. When they advertise on television, they are able to obtain estimates of the audience to their individual commercials at the times and on the days they are broadcast.

Print is therefore seen by many advertisers as offering less accountability for their investment, especially as titles sprout more and more sections and pages, arguably making individual advertisements less and less likely to attract every person who buys or reads a publication.

Print audience research depends on people being asked to remember what they have read. In contrast, television audience research employs meters attached to the television set so that people don't have to remember what they watched (although they may in fact not be watching, even when the audience measurement data says they are).

Given the thousands of advertisements that run in the print media, it would hardly be reasonable to ask respondents to remember every ad they were exposed to or, even for ads they did recall, to remember on which pages of which publications they saw them.

Recall of individual advertisements will, in any case, be dependent on much more than the page number or section in which the ad appeared – such as the quality of the creative execution – arguably not the responsibility of syndicated research to measure.

Admeasure

In response to this perceived gap in print audience research, MRI in the United States announced the launch of its Admeasure service in June 2009, designed to integrate readership estimates from three different sources:

- Readership data from its main survey, a face-to-face study of 26,000 adults covering standard average issue readership estimates for major magazines;
- Estimates of issue-specific variation in readership culled from a separate on-line panel of 5,000 adults;
- Ad readership scores from its Starch service, which uses several methods to interview readers about their reading and noting of individual advertisements in specific magazine issues.

The goal of the service is to generate audience estimates – and the actions people say they take as a result of seeing these specific ads – for any print advertisement greater than one third of a page appearing in specific issues of more than 100 consumer magazines.

At the time of writing, findings from this service were unavailable. But, if successful, it may prove a model for helping to make readership measurement more relevant to marketers and publishers.

Engagement measures

But while most print audience measurement services report on the number and composition of readers of 'average' issues and fail to identify audiences to individual advertisements, there are plenty of ways in which the data can be – and are – supplemented.

Newspapers and magazines both play to a number of important strengths as advertising media that go beyond simple counts of the number of people reading or looking at them.

Media planners and buyers will use their own experience and judgement in moving beyond raw readership data. But the widespread need to put hard numbers on marketing plans to provide accountability suggests a continuing need for research that can be used to guide and support media placement decisions.

Judgements need to be made on how attentively and how intensively people read. These judgements will, in turn, be influenced by where and when they read, by the reading topic and by their 'relationship' with a magazine (is it, for example, a favourite they subscribe to or one they just picked up in a waiting room?).

One of the particular strengths highlighted by the print media is that of audience 'engagement'. It is perfectly possible, for example, for somebody to be in a room or environment with a television or radio blaring away without them paying any conscious attention it. It is very hard to read without at least some level of engagement.

Much work has been undertaken to probe the reading experience. This includes looking at the time people spend reading, the sections or parts of a publication they read, the proportion of an issue seen, how carefully or how long readers look at advertisements or simply the importance of a newspaper or magazine in their daily lives – all of which can be used to enrich the raw readership numbers.

Plenty of research has been carried out into the readership of individual sections of newspapers,[29] which have mushroomed in recent years. Unsurprisingly, this work invariably shows there to be fewer people reading any given section or page in a newspaper than there are total readers of the title.

Such findings are naturally seized on by agencies to demand discounts off rates which have been historically determined by the total readership. Even though publishers may respond that individual sections offer better targeting opportunities and higher engagement, large numbers often win the day.

To the extent this is true, publishers may find it difficult to justify investing money in such research, even though it is clearly in the interests of more accurate data overall. In the event, only a handful of countries – including the UK – have actually incorporated section readership into their standard audience surveys.

Attempts have also been made to look at the impact of placing advertising within specific editorial.[30]

The UK *Quality of Reading Study*, carried out both in 1997/98 and in 1999/2000 sought to measure a range of 'quality' indicators[31] across both newspapers and magazines including time spent reading, proportion of pages opened, agreement with certain attitude statements (e.g. 'I look forward to reading it') and the likelihood that people would take any actions as a result of reading a publication (e.g. 'bought something'). Plenty of variation between magazine genres and individual titles was found in the research.

68 of the 95 readership surveys examined in a recent global compilation[32] of print research contained qualitative measures of one sort or another, although the depth and extent of these varied considerably.

The US Magazine Involvement Alliance set out to discover whether a connection existed between key qualitative indicators and advertising recall.[33] Their study concluded that the ad itself often correlated most strongly with recall, but that metrics like time spent reading were also important.

Affinity Research's VISTA Print Effectiveness Rating Service, also from the USA, confirms a strong connection between reader involvement in a magazine (e.g. 'it is one of my favourites') and both recall of advertising and propensity to 'take action'.[34]

It is worth pointing out, finally, that advertisements tend to 'wear out' faster in magazines than they do in other media like television.[35] Magazines are a medium where people can choose to spend as little or as much time as they want with individual advertisements – when they have taken a message on board, therefore, they will arguably only want to spend limited time reading the same message again. For these reasons planners may want to consider whether running the same copy for long periods of time is effective and whether, indeed, running multiple copies in a single campaign would pay dividends.

But it is also worth mentioning that the print media are arguably under less threat from new ad-avoidance technologies than their rivals in television, radio and the internet. Readers have always been able to turn the page when they are no longer interested in something; viewers are only just beginning to embrace these powers with intrusive media like television.[36]

Other print research

Industry readership studies provide media planners and buyers with a 'currency' for trading space. They do not differentiate between the multiple ways newspaper or magazine advertising can be deployed. No account is taken, for example, of the size of the space bought (i.e. a double-page spread, a page, a half-page etc.) nor of the advertisement's position in the publication.

Instead, planners are simply presented with estimates of how many people see or look into each title as a whole. From this they must make their own judgements as to whether readers are more or less likely to see advertising in certain positions or whether the size of the execution makes any difference.

Research has been carried out in various countries into whether pages, double-page spreads or fractional sizes are more effective or whether ads are more impactful in different parts of a paper. Rates charged for space vary by both position and size – so clearly advantage can be gained by exploiting any difference between relative rates and impact.

Other factors that have shown themselves to be important determinants of advertising impact in newspapers include the degree of advertising clutter in a given spread, the interest of readers in the product category,[37] the power of individual creative ideas and executions and how long a particular ad has been running.

Typical measures of impact used in the various studies include page traffic, advertising recall, ad 'noting', ad association or attribution and ad 'reading'. Page traffic represents the percentage of readers who have opened a given spread. Ad noting is a measure of whether readers recognise having seen an ad, while reading refers to whether they have actually read some or all of it (sometimes collected as 'read some' or 'read most').

The billetts consultancy in the UK used advertising recall as their key measure of effectiveness in a 2001[38] study of national newspaper advertising. People were invited into a central location after being screened for demographics and whether they had read particular issues of various newspapers. They were then physically taken through these titles.

Respondents were asked questions about how they read as well as about recall of individual advertisements. The average reader was able to recall over 53 individual advertisements in each issue they read with average advertising recall of 22%. Position was important, with ads in the first quartile scoring the highest. But contrary to industry belief, little difference was found between left- and right-hand positions. The size of the ad did matter.

The research also confirmed the adverse impact of clutter: newspapers with more pages and more advertisements tended to attract lower average advertising recall. Interestingly, this was the opposite of what has been found for magazine advertising.[39] But the findings did confirm that colour advertising, while generating higher impact, did not justify the premiums being charged at the time. Finally, interest in the product category being advertised was an important factor, as would be expected, though no account was taken of the length of time any particular copy had been running.

A large-scale Dutch study reported that size had a big influence on people's attention to advertising, although its relative influence was less when it came to message comprehension.[40]

Research by European publishers in the 1970s and 1980s, confirmed by later agency studies, showed consistently that larger sizes tended to score more highly on measures such as 'scanned' or 'read', although diminishing returns tended to set in fairly early – i.e. a double-page spread scored more highly than a page, but not twice as high; a page was not twice as impactful as a half-page and so on.[41]

US organisations like GfK Starch, Gallup & Robinson and Affinity VISTA have established systematic measures of consumer receptivity to individual advertisements in consumer and trade magazines. This is done through interviewing readers either face-to-face, via mail or on-line about their exposure to, and experience of, individual magazine advertisements. The results of thousands of interviews are then aggregated into 'norms' which allow media planners to gauge the relative impact of different magazine genres, ad positions and so on.

Starch in the United States occasionally produces summaries of its findings. For example, in one such compilation, looking at 'ad noting' (the percentage of readers who say they have seen any part of an ad) the company concluded:

- *There is little difference between left- and right-hand positions;*
- *The impact of size varies by product category.* For example, the differential impact of a double-page spread versus that of a page is greater in the toiletries category than for financial services;
- *Position in magazines has almost no impact on ad noting.*

A Belgian magazine study, the stop/watch report,[42] summarised nine years of research findings, concluding that:

- *The bigger the ad, the greater the impact* – but this difference is not as great as the difference in size (e.g. a page is 55% – not 100% – more effective than a half-page);
- *Covers are more effective than ordinary pages.* The later in the issue the better;
- *'Creative' formats are more impactful than standard 'flat' advertising.* These include such devices as gatefolds, inserts, pop-ups, scent samples and so on;
- *The difference between left- and right-hand positions is negligible;*
- *Position in the magazine (front, middle or back) has almost no difference on impact.*

Affinity LLC, which operates the VISTA Print Effectiveness Rating Service, comes to pretty much the same conclusions as the two studies already quoted.[43]

The future

Newspapers and magazines are still significant industries, with millions of people relying on them for news, entertainment and information.

But the economic model, for newspapers in particular, is changing. A long time ago, newspapers were the principal source of news for most people. Radio and television challenged this primacy, but did not destroy the medium.

Consumers today can now control the news they receive – both what they read and when they read it. With free content having been on the internet for more than a decade, they are unlikely to be keen on paying for the privilege of receiving news they previously obtained for nothing.

It is possible that newspapers might provide something exclusive and indispensable to them. Or that the strength of their brands might keep readers coming to them as 'default' sources of news and information. In this, both magazines and newspapers are showing some success.

To take an example from the United States, it is clear that newspaper websites have been very successful in attracting readers – in the first quarter of 2009, Nielsen Online and the Newspaper Association of America (NAA)[44] reported that they attracted more than 73.3 million monthly unique visitors on average – 44% of all internet users. This was 10.5% higher than in the same period of 2008.

In addition, newspaper website visitors generated more than 3.5 billion page views per month throughout the quarter, an increase of 12.8% over the same period the year before. These figures are the highest for any quarter since the NAA began tracking the data in 2004.

A compilation of Nielsen Online data by the Magazine Publishers Association, also in the United States, noted that 76 million people visited one or other of 476 magazine websites in the first quarter of 2009, up more than 7% from the previous year.[45]

Almost 60% of UK internet users accessed newspaper websites in March 2009 according to the Newspaper Marketing Agency, with the most popular section visited being the news.

The vast majority of these websites are free to access. But while web audiences are rising, the number of people who pay to buy newspapers is falling in many countries. Newspapers and magazines make substantial amounts of money from the cover prices they charge. With this revenue now declining alongside advertising revenue – hit by the recession as well as the migration of classified advertising to the web – their financial future looks parlous.

Recently, the World Association of Newspapers suggested four possible futures for the newspaper business, based on extreme scenarios that looked at (a) whether or not the mass market would still exist in 2020 and (b) whether or not traditional media brands like the *New York Times* or the *Financial Times* would still be the principal trusted sources of news. Four scenarios were developed looking at the various combinations of possibilities and were named after James Bond films:[46]

1 *For Your Eyes Only* conjured up a world where consumers spurn mass media and use technology to customise their access to content. In short, the oft-spoken 'death of newspapers'.
2 *Diamonds are Forever* envisaged newspaper brands adapting successfully to fragmenting consumer needs, but no longer serving a mass market as it currently exists.
3 *Die Another Day* assumes that the mass market will not disappear and that newspaper brands would still have a place as trusted sources of news, but that the delivery platforms will not be the same as they are today; in short, that the internet and mobile would take over from paper.
4 *Thunderball* pictures a world which still features a mass market, but finds newspapers unable to adapt effectively to the new technology platforms.

Undoubtedly, as new technology takes root and people make increasing use of their ability to customise how they receive news, sports information and more, both newspapers and magazines will have to adapt.

Many print brands already distribute content via multiple platforms: in the traditional print format, via websites, television programmes, radio podcasts, blogs, mobile 'apps' and more.

Advertisers will want to understand whether and how the values of a traditional print brand carry over to other distribution platforms and which platforms people are more or less attentive to.

Print audience measurement will need to focus, as one commentator noted, 'on the size of a newspaper's footprint in a reader's life and whether or not readers turn to newspaper (brands) when making buying decisions'.[47]

The very definition of 'readership' as refined over many years in the syndicated surveys will have to change. Traditional readership surveys, carried out face-to-face, with relatively small samples of the population, will not be sufficient on their own to fully capture the new world of print content measurement. But they will undoubtedly continue to play a part in the medium's future.

3 Measuring Out of Home audiences

Introduction

Officially, around $31.4 billion was spent by advertisers in the Out of Home medium in 2008.[1] This is almost certainly an under-estimate.

Out of Home media – or Outdoor as it is sometimes known in the UK – is all around us, embracing much of the advertising we come across when we are travelling to work, shopping or at leisure.

Statistics on the industry – and much of the audience measurement activity – are largely confined to measuring roadside panels and public transport networks. Yet much of the dynamism of the Out of Home business over the past decade has come from the explosion of what are sometimes called 'ambient' formats.[2] These can include advertising on ashtrays, beer mats, mugs, sandwich boards, balloons, airships, petrol pumps, floors, doors, litter bins, bus shelters, supermarket trolleys, milk cartons, the backs of supermarket receipts and bus tickets.

Outside the home, consumers can be exposed to advertising messages by the roadside, in airports, train stations, bus depots, taxi stands, filling stations, sports stadiums, public restrooms, lifts, shopping malls, telephone kiosks, inside and outside supermarkets, in fields as they drive past on the highway and much besides.

Advertising can even be digitally projected onto panels at sports events or onto the pitch itself – although these are ads that only television viewers will see.

The medium plays to a number of strengths for advertisers.[3] These include:

- It is pure advertising, with little or no editorial context.
- Ubiquity – it can appear anywhere, although it is primarily an urban medium.

- 24/7 presence – it can be seen before, during and after shopping.
- Non-intrusive – it does not interrupt people in their daily lives.
- Flexibility – some electronic sites can be updated or changed several times a day. Technology has also enabled a growing range of digital enhancements (e.g. moving images).
- Targeting – it can be located to reach a specific audience.

But for the audience researcher, Out of Home presents a number of very unique challenges. Not the least of these is the very fact that it carries no 'editorial' as such. Unlike newspapers or television, people do not purposefully buy or watch Out of Home media. Contact with it is simply part of the backdrop to their daily lives.

As a result, it is as difficult for people to remember how many Out of Home advertising contacts they had yesterday as it would be to recall how many cars passed them or how many of the cars were Fiats. Yet they probably will remember at least something about which newspapers they read or which television programmes they watched.

Another challenge is the sheer size and diversity of the medium. No individual has exactly the same pattern of travel outside the home – exposure to Out of Home advertising will be unique to each person. In a similar vein, no particular poster or supermarket trolley is likely to have the same number of people being exposed to it in any given week.

A further challenge is to assess the closeness between somebody's *opportunity* to see a poster or other Out of Home advertisement and actual exposure. This issue arises in all audience research. Television viewers are usually counted if they are recorded as being present in a room with a television set switched on. Magazine or newspaper readers are reported as having an opportunity to see an advertisement if they see any issue of a particular title carrying the ad.

In all these cases, opportunities to see advertising are not the same as actual exposure to it. But the link between driving past a poster and seeing it, or between riding on a bus and noticing a particular advertising panel is even less direct. Audience measures have to address all of these issues.

Early history of Out of Home media

Posters as we see them today date back to 1870, when the printing industry mastered chromolithography, a chemical process which removed the need to use raised surfaces on a printing plate in order for letters or images to be reproduced. The technique enabled mass production of posters in colour.

A noted early exponent of poster advertising was Jules Chéret, who created posters for Parisian theatres and music halls and went on to produce advertisements for a range of drinks, perfumes, soaps, cosmetics and pharmaceutical products. He made several contributions to the technical process which were to make rapid colour printing in volume possible. He also played a major role in the transformation of the creative role of posters, giving them an identity distinct from other visual arts. Eventually, Chéret became a major advertising force, adding the railroad companies and a number of manufacturing businesses to his client list.

The modern industry

Few countries provide an accurate count of the number of posters and advertising panels available on the roadside, in train and bus stations, on taxi sides or in supermarkets, let alone how many balloons, milk cartons, beer mats or shop signs exist.

Yet this has not stopped commentators and journalists touting 'facts' and 'research' which claim that consumers are exposed to 5,000 advertisements a day (Google records 17 million hits for the phrase '5,000 ads a day'). It is likely – if anybody were to really count the number of brand advertisements they passed as they went about their daily life in any large city – that the number would indeed be very high (although this particular number has never been validated).

The shop signs people pass are advertisements. The buses, taxis, lorries and vans driving past them on the street often feature advertising messages or brand mentions. Arguably, the vehicles themselves are advertisements for the particular brand being driven. Posters are present on buildings and inside shopping malls. The backs of bus tickets and ATM receipts may also contain messages. There are clearly far too many to count and too many for any individual to take in.

POSTAR, the UK's audience measurement organisation, offers audience estimates on more than 240,000 roadside panels across the country.[4]

Statistics from the State Administration of Industry and Commerce in China counted no fewer than 69,000 outdoor advertising *companies* in 2004, with a combined inventory which could well be even higher than the US number.[5]

The Outdoor Advertising Association of America listed more than 1.1 million Out of Home displays in 2008 (in addition to uncounted displays such as on phone kiosks, newsracks, arenas and stadia and so on), broken down as shown in Table 3.1.[6]

Ambient outdoor advertising

When entrepreneur Richard Branson launched his Virgin Cola brand in the United States, he began by driving a Second World War tank through Times Square in New York. At the Virgin Brides wedding service launch there he donned a $10,000 white silk bridal gown. In Australia he flew into a press conference hanging from a helicopter promising to save Australians from their money-grabbing mobile contractors.

He is not the only one doing it. Early in 2006, Nelson's Column in London carried advertising for the first time during the monument's renovation. There are countless other examples of 'guerrilla' marketing, as it is sometimes known.

Media stunts can be an integral part of a brand campaign. They are designed to make people sit up and notice and to generate as many

Table 3.1 Number of Out of Home display faces, 2008

Billboards	Street furniture	Transit
Bulletins: 159,485	Bus shelters: 43,995	Buses: 340,777
Digital bulletins: 1,500	Shopping malls: 40,734	Airports: 61,690
Posters: 165,528		Subway & rail: 219,645
Junior posters: 33,158		Truckside/mobile: 8,879
Walls/Spectaculars: 1,697		Taxis/wrapped vehicles: 50,239

column inches of news coverage as possible. Usually, however, they are one-off events.

What is known as 'ambient' media in the UK can also embrace the execution of creative media ideas over longer periods. Dictionary.com defines ambient as: 'completely surrounding; encompassing'. But if the words remain primarily in British usage, the practice of placing marketing messages in unusual or eye-catching places outside the home is a global one. As traditional media lose influence and become more cluttered with advertising, the quest for attention-grabbing strategies continues.

Attempts were made in the late 1990s[7] to classify the kinds of activity that came under the ambient heading according to the environment where consumers might come into contact with them. For example:

- *Retail*: shopping trolleys, floors, car park ads, receipts, shopping bags, in-store TV;
- *Leisure*: postcard racks, beer mats/coasters, advertising in sports centres/fitness clubs;
- *Travel*: lorry, bus and taxi sides, airport ramps, petrol/gas pump nozzles, car park barriers;
- *Other*: balloons, aerial writing, airships, video screens, litter bins, milk cartons, bookmarks, fridge magnets.

Audience measurement

With such a diverse range of formats, it is perhaps unsurprising that Out of Home has, at least historically, been one of the least well-researched advertising mediums, with many countries having next to no comprehensive estimates even of roadside poster audiences.

Where audience data was produced, it was often used sparingly. Media planners were sceptical of the vast numbers generated in comparison with other media – it would not be unusual for a poster campaign to 'reach' 90% of the population an average of perhaps 30 times in a major city using a definition such as 'passing' a site. This is because a raw count of passages past a site does not take account of the strong likelihood that people will not (indeed could not) always be looking intently at every panel they pass.

For Out of Home media to generate credible audience estimates they need to address at least four important challenges:

1   First, it is a good idea to have a central database identifying the exact location of all the sites needing to be measured, preferably with detailed information about the type of environment where the sites are (e.g. the type of road and whether it is in a residential, commercial or retail district).

2   Second, estimates need to be made of the number of people driving or walking past every site over a given period of time.

3   Third, an Out of Home measurement system must offer a way of estimating the probability that any given population will have of being exposed to a campaign using the medium – i.e. across multiple panels and over time.

4   Finally, 'passing by' a site does not guarantee people will look at it. Ways of adjusting gross passages downwards to allow for the differing contact probability and visibility of each panel need to be developed.

1. Mapping the poster sites

Simply knowing and recording the location of all the panels in a market is not as straightforward as it might seem, although many countries have made progress on this in recent years, particularly with the development of digital mapping technology.

An early example was the UK's OSCAR. Launched in 1985, following several years of work, the Outdoor Site Classification and Audience Research project set out to compile – for the first time in Britain – a complete listing and classification of all the roadside and outdoor retail poster sites in the country.

Because of the high cost of undertaking such a comprehensive census, it was important to capture as much data as possible on each site visit – data that would be useful for media planners and sales teams in gauging the quality and visibility of each panel. So, apart from establishing the precise location of every site on their visit, researchers also recorded:

*   The number and size of different panels at the site;
*   The type of location (e.g. whether it was in a major or minor shopping area, residential or commercial district etc.);
*   Information about the kind of road it was on (i.e. a main road, side street, highway etc.);

- Data on the site's basic physical characteristics: for example, was the panel angled towards on-coming traffic or side-on? Could it be seen by traffic travelling in both directions? How high up was it? Was it illuminated?;
- Details on the traffic flow past the site, including a two-minute traffic count;
- Its proximity to retailers and other infrastructure.

Collecting all these data is a necessary first step to creating the kind of end-to-end audience measurement services that now exist to varying degrees in the UK, the USA, Germany, Denmark, Ireland, the Netherlands, Norway, Finland, France, Switzerland, Belgium and Australia.

2. Counting vehicular and pedestrian traffic

Once the location of all the sites to be measured is known, the next step is to find out how many people pass by these sites, either on foot or in vehicles.

This does not always need special research to be undertaken. Often, local transport authorities carry out regular traffic surveys to assist with planning, which involve estimating the volume of traffic on various roads. These surveys can also be drawn on by the poster industry in many instances to provide estimates of the number of people passing by their sites.

Over many years, for example, the vehicle counts made by the US Department of Transportation were the basis for 'Daily Effective Circulation' or DEC estimates, the principal currency of poster buying and selling in the United States.

An obvious drawback of the surveys is that they don't count the number of pedestrians walking by, only the vehicle traffic. Neither do they count the number of occupants in the vehicles. The studies, as well, can become dated if they are not carried out regularly.

More recently, a range of automatic traffic counting devices have been installed in many countries, at least on major roads, enabling more accurate and up-to-date figures to be used to count the traffic past some sites.

Where up-to-date automatic counts are not available, it is possible for researchers to physically count vehicle and pedestrian traffic at a sample of locations and to project these counts to cover other locations.

Modelling traffic counts

In the UK, long before automatic traffic-counting devices were as widespread as they are today, OSCAR created a model to estimate both vehicular and pedestrian traffic past each site.

To do this, a sample of 437 locations around the country were selected to be representative of all sites, based on the information collected during the original site census. At each of these locations, detailed counts were made of the number of vehicles and pedestrians passing by and combined with the findings from previous government research (which provided estimates of the average number of occupants in each vehicle).

The counts were analysed alongside some of the other data collected during the site census (e.g. on the district, road type and local population), enabling statisticians to build a model which could predict the traffic and pedestrian counts for any site in the country on the basis of its particular geographical characteristics.

So, for example, an estimate of vehicle numbers could be made for an individual site by looking at information on the type of town it was in, how far it was from the town centre, its distance to the next town, the type of road it was on and the two-minute traffic count. Pedestrian traffic was estimated using other factors, such as the population of the town, what kind of area it was in and so on.

Through these means, the gross number of passages past every poster panel in the OSCAR database could be estimated.

3. Measuring Out of Home campaign reach and frequency

Whether the numbers come from local authority traffic counts or are derived from a model, they still don't tell marketers anything about the demographics of the people passing or about how many people see various *combinations* of sites over the course of a day or week. A poster campaign can consist of tens, hundreds or even thousands of individual panels – and it is these campaigns that marketers need to assess.

To meet these needs, the kind of site-centric measurement described above needs to be complemented with measurement of people. Specifically, how often do people leave their homes, where do they go and what chances are there that they will pass a given poster or group of posters over the course of a day or week?

The first travel survey which set out to answer these questions was fielded in the United States in 1946 on behalf of the Traffic Audit Bureau.[8] The study consisted of a series of in-home interviews in Fort Wayne, Indiana where people were asked where they had been when travelling outside the home on the previous day. It found that three-quarters of adults left their homes on an average day and therefore had the potential to pass by a poster site.

A year later, a follow-up study was conducted in Cedar Rapids, Iowa, this time in the form of a 30-day travel diary. Results indicated that almost everybody left their homes at some point during the period, although, as Brian Copland pointed out when reviewing the study: 'Of the eight who did not go outdoors at all, three were permanent invalids, one was in hospital and one was in jail the entire 30 days.'[9]

The first UK survey, in 1952, asked 5,359 people in nine towns about their travel behaviour over a one-week period, using maps as prompts.[10] At this time, posters tended to be bought and sold on a city-by-city, town-by-town basis.

Since then, travel surveys have played a major part in the Out of Home measurement systems in many countries, some of which are detailed below. It is worth pointing out, however, that there are a number of inherent limitations involved in using them to estimate the reach and frequency of Out of Home campaigns:

1 The sample can never be large enough to accurately capture passages past every Out of Home site;
2 People may not accurately recall their travel behaviour, especially over an extended period;
3 Response is likely to be poor to surveys which demand a large amount of detailed information over a long period.

As has been pointed out by transport researchers, travel is a non-random activity, depending as it does on where each individual lives, where he works and which modes of transport he tends to use. It is almost as unique to an individual as his fingerprints.

To match every individual poster site location to a large enough number of individuals, each with unique travel behaviour, would require very large samples – one estimate just for the city of Chicago, for example, went as high as 285,000 people.[11] This would clearly be impractical for a whole country.

Modelling reach and frequency: the Copland formula

Given these limitations, it is clearly necessary to introduce some way of projecting travel survey findings from an economically viable sample of people onto the population as a whole. This was recognised early on.

Brian Copland, who had directed the 1952 UK research, noted that there was a statistical relationship between a town's population and the likely audience to a poster campaign.

It was, and is, fairly obvious that if 50 posters are put up in a small and a large town, the likelihood of seeing one of the posters is going to be greater for somebody living in the small town than it is for an individual living in the larger town. What was perhaps less obvious was that the relationship would be quite so regular. Copland was able to estimate the rate at which a poster campaign's coverage of a town's population would build simply by knowing its population.

What he called the 'A value' – the average number of times an average person in a town would pass an average site – could be multiplied by the number of sites posted there to yield a weekly audience ratings estimate. To calculate the percentage of individuals reached he came up with the following formula:

$$C = (A * S) / \{(A * S) + B\}$$

where C = net coverage, A = the A value, S = the number of sites, and $B = 4$ (a constant).

The results were groundbreaking at the time and the Copland formula for estimating outdoor coverage and frequency became the basis of poster planning in the UK and many other countries for most of the rest of the twentieth century.

But the formula, while simple, had a number of obvious weaknesses. For example, it assumed an even distribution of panels within a town – whereas it was more likely that panels would be concentrated in certain areas.

Once campaign planning went beyond town borders and started looking at wider regions, it became harder to calculate the A value. Neither was it adapted to looking at particular target audiences within the population.

Another drawback was that campaigns nearly always ran for longer than a single week – the basis for Copland's reach calculation. And finally, of course, there is no such thing as an 'average' site – all will differ in both their physical and environmental situations.

Modelling travel behaviour

So, with the world having moved on, other methods needed to be found for addressing the limitations of travel surveys. One approach was to create a detailed picture of travel behaviour using two separate surveys.

In the Netherlands, travel surveys covering around 10,000 respondents had historically been used to obtain reach, frequency and demographic estimates. In the late 1990s, a new approach, known as 'route reconstruction' was introduced.

The idea[12] was to take the responses from a large-scale survey of people's travel behaviour carried out continuously by the government and to combine it with data from a smaller, but far more detailed survey.

The larger survey, carried out by the Dutch Central Bureau of Statistics, quizzed respondents about the source and destination of all the journeys taken during the course of a single day, the purpose of each trip and the mode of transport used. No information was collected on the routes people had taken.

The second, smaller study was first carried out face-to-face in 1998 amongst 7,000 respondents, asking in detail about their travel behaviour the previous day.

A model was then built with the goal of predicting the routes the larger sample would take between their known origins and destinations. A range of possibilities were considered such as the shortest route, the quickest or the one with the fewest junctions. These were then compared with the actual route data collected in the second survey.

It turned out, unsurprisingly, that people did not always take either the quickest or the shortest routes. The model was able to generate probabilities for each type of route and to compare that with the demographic characteristics of people, their journey purpose, the day of the week and so on.

It was found to be reasonably accurate in predicting actual journeys (where known from the smaller survey) and could be used in conjunction with the known location of panels to help media planners estimate the audiences to their poster campaigns.

In the United States a similar model was developed by the Traffic Audit Bureau (TAB) in 2008. It began with short mail surveys in 15 different markets to establish the destination and purpose of journeys outside the home. A more detailed face-to-face survey was carried out in five markets to gather data on the detailed routes taken by people to their destinations over the course of a week.

The model allowed the number of trips and likely destinations to be projected to all 200 local markets in the country. It used secondary sources such as the US census to establish journey-to-work and place-of-work statistics for every region, as well as population data. These were seen in the surveys to be the principal influences on people's travel patterns.

Likely routes were modelled using data from the detailed survey and overlaid with the poster sites located on these routes, allowing audience estimates to be built for every panel.

GPS

By 2009 a more advanced form of travel survey was beginning to take root. This was the practice of equipping a sample of respondents with Global Positioning System (GPS) devices to automatically gather travel information, without them needing to remember where they had been or the routes they had taken.

GPS, originally developed by the United States Department of Defense, involves the transmission of radio waves by a group of satellites orbiting above the earth. A GPS receiving device detects signals from several of these satellites and is able, using the information on the distance between them and the times the signals are transmitted and received, to calculate its precise geographical position on a continuous basis.

Using this technology, it is therefore possible to identify the exact location of people carrying such a device and to relate it to the known geographical location of any Out of Home site.

The earliest usage of GPS to measure Out of Home audiences was initiated in Denmark by the poster contractor J.C. Decaux. In Germany, piloting and field testing of a GPS device were carried out in 2004 and

2005; work then took place on linking the data generated by the GPS to a telephone survey on travel outside the home the following year.

GPS measurement has since been piloted or adopted as a component in Out of Home measurement systems in Italy, the Netherlands, Switzerland, South Africa, the United States and other countries.[13]

In the UK, the largest GPS-equipped panel to date, consisting of 10,000 people carrying the devices, started fieldwork in 2009 – with results expected in 2010.

But while GPS has addressed the limitation of respondent memory – asking them to recall the details of all journeys taken over a period of time – it has not addressed that of sample size. It is simply not economically viable to field a large enough sample of device carriers to measure every poster site or every person's likely exposure to Out of Home media.

A model therefore needs to be created that will use the output from the GPS and/or travel survey alongside traffic counts and any other relevant information to generate audience estimates that cover every site.

4. Contact probability

Before we consider how the various survey components involved in Out of Home measurement are linked together, one other component of the measurement needs to be addressed – that of contact probability.

As the UK OSCAR work found, simply counting or estimating the number of people and cars passing by each poster did not tell the whole story. Some posters could be more easily seen than others. Many of the physical characteristics of each site noted during the census exercise would clearly influence the ease with which people could come into contact with each panel.

As a result, a procedure was developed in the UK for refining the likely exposure contact of the audiences to each site according to a number of criteria. They included factors listed in Table 3.2.

A number of countries including the Netherlands, Australia, the USA, Germany, the Nordic countries, Ireland, Belgium and Switzerland employ variations of the OSCAR approach, applying data on the physical characteristics of a site to adjust gross passages past a site downwards to allow for factors likely to affect its contact probability.

Table 3.2 Vehicular and pedestrian visibility

Vehicular visibility	Pedestrian visibility
Distance at which visible	Proportion able to see panel (judgement by fieldworker)
Angle to road	Competition from other panels
Competition from other panels	Illumination
Deflection from line of site	
Degree of obstruction	
Height of panel from ground	
Illumination	

Source: Derek Bloom: 'The audience to outdoor posters' in Raymond Kent (ed.) *Measuring Media Audiences*, 1994

Visibility Adjusted Impacts (VAIs)

Much of the adjustment to contact probabilities in the original OSCAR approach subsequently has been based on the judgement of fieldworkers, asked to record the ease with which they could see panels from various angles and distances.

The next stage in the evolution of visibility studies was to try to gauge what consumers actually did see – to quantify the effect of each of these factors on a poster's visibility – i.e. the size of the panel, its distance from the road or pavement, its height and angle, whether or not it was illuminated and so on.[14]

To address this, a group of people in the UK were equipped with special headsets allowing everything they looked at to be tracked and measured. They were asked to view a number of photographs from perspectives as drivers, passengers or pedestrians. Altogether some 63,000 pieces of eye-movement data were gathered. The result was a much lower – albeit arguably more realistic – estimate of a poster campaign's likelihood of being seen.

Eye-tracking studies were not new, though none had been as comprehensive as this. As long ago as 1954, in a US experiment, an electrically operated camera was actually hooked up behind a poster to count how many sets of eyes could be seen as a way to compute exposure. Numerous other studies have been carried out in the USA since the

1970s focusing on the medium's ability to actually be looked at by passing motorists and passengers.

Many countries, including the USA with its 'Eyes On' approach, have now incorporated visibility adjustments into their poster audience data.

Linking it all together

It is worth looking at how some countries have succeeded in integrating the various components of Out of Home measurement noted earlier. These include the traffic counts at each site, the surveys of behaviour and details on the location and characteristics of each site.

In essence, the various datasets must be linked so that a user of the audience measurement service can estimate how many and what types of people pass by any given panel or group of panels containing a particular campaign and how likely they are to be exposed to the campaign message featured on the panels.

The mathematics of such an exercise are complex. But broadly speaking, some individual sites will have been passed by enough people taking part in the travel survey or involved in the GPS measurement to have generated a mathematical probability score for different members of the population. As well as this, detailed count data from automatic counting stations will have been collected for these sites.

Other sites may not only have the counts, but will also have information about their location, type of area, local population and so on which enable probabilities to be estimated based on these characteristics.

As can be seen in the following examples, many countries now incorporate a number of different types of data into their audience measurement services.

Germany

In Germany, the research organisation ag.ma has, since 2007, combined several sources of information to create audience estimates for each poster panel:

1 A nationally representative telephone survey covering 21,000 individuals. Respondents are questioned about journeys outside the home on the previous day, including the start, end and

intermediate points on the journeys, as well as the means of transport and purpose of the trip;

2 Just under 9,000 people carry a GPS meter with them when they travel outside their homes, for a total of seven days;

3 Estimates of vehicular and pedestrian traffic in towns and cities of more than 10,000 inhabitants are taken from a separate database;

4 Details of the physical characteristics of each panel and how they are likely to affect contact probability are collected.

The Netherlands

A new Dutch system, under the auspices of the Platform Buitenreclame Exploitanten (PBE), is scheduled to be released in Q2 2010. It comprises:

1 Classification and mapping of all roadside, retail and transit and bus panel sites according to various environmental and physical criteria;

2 A national travel survey covering 7,400 respondents, detailing their travel behaviour over a short period of time;

3 A GPS device placed with 2,600 people who carry it for 14 days;

4 Adaptation of the UK Visibility Adjustment model to refine audience estimates.

The UK

The launch of POSTAR in the UK in 1996 sought to build and improve on the various OSCAR features, bringing together all the elements necessary to create credible audience estimates for each poster panel.[15] Six components were involved:[16]

1 Traffic counts;

2 Pedestrian counts;

3 Reach calculation;

4 Dispersion factor;

5 Visibility adjusted impacts (VAIs); and

6 Refinements.

The first two steps took data from official, local authority figures (initially incorporating traffic counts covering 10,000 roads and 9,000 pedestrian counts), while the third and fourth were partially sourced from traffic surveys.

VAIs were applied to the gross data and further adjustments made on the basis of physical factors such as whether the panel was illuminated.

Other Out of Home media

But hundreds of other media – including the ambient media examples listed earlier and many more – cannot offer systematic audience estimates.

Services introduced in the United States in the latter part of 2006 sought to bring the OTS (opportunities to see) approach into the retail arena. For example Arbitron and Scarborough Research launched the *Mall Shopper Audience Data* service so marketers could measure how many and what kinds of people visit specific shopping malls and are potentially exposed to their messages there.

A consortium of major US retailers and manufacturers developed a method known as *PRISM* to measure in-store journeys and, in turn, shopper OTS for each aisle in a store (although this service was closed in early 2009). The system used infra-red beams to track shoppers' movements which were then compared with sales data, producing a measure of the performance of in-store sales tools such as shelf location and promotional displays.

Engagement measures

Many attempts have been made over the years to demonstrate that people do notice poster advertising when they pass by.

One example from the UK in the 1980s involved a 'spoof' advertising campaign. A picture of a small girl contained the caption: 'My name is Amy and I like slugs and snails'. It had no particular meaning and was not selling a product.* But following the campaign, awareness levels of the campaign 'message' were very high, demonstrating on behalf of the poster industry that if the message was noticeable, people would remember it.

Another consideration is that of 'dwell time'. People waiting for trains on the London Underground, for example, tend to be exposed to poster advertising on the platform for several minutes compared with perhaps

---

* In fact, Amy was the daughter of the sales director of the large poster contractor, More O'Ferrall, which sponsored the research.

fleeting opportunities if they are walking or driving by a roadside site. Research commissioned by a transport contractor in the UK showed that people were more likely to remember and to be engaged with advertising messages to which they were exposed for longer periods.[17]

Over the next few years – particularly as more and more countries digest the impact of new electronic measurement approaches – an important challenge for the medium will be to ensure that outdoor media is fully integrated into advertisers' market mix models.

This is a challenge also being faced by other traditional media such as radio and print, which have not been as effectively integrated into these models as has television. Only then can the actual business impact of Out of Home's contribution be assessed effectively.

Another goal of the industry should be to integrate all other forms of outdoor media into the measurement process for the first time. GPS now allows this.

The future

The Out of Home medium has made major steps forward in its audience measurement approach in recent years. This may be partly because there is less history to challenge and therefore fewer vested interests to oppose change.

An important landmark for the industry has been the publication, in 2009, of a comprehensive set of global guidelines[18] detailing 'best practice' in Out-of-Home audience measurement, guidelines which a growing number of countries already follow.

Nevertheless, most of the changes have tended towards reducing reported audiences versus those claimed historically, while increasing the cost of measurement – a brave but necessary step for the medium to take in its on-going competitive battle with other media.

It will be interesting to see to see how many other markets bite the bullet and move forward towards more accurate – and expensive – audience measurement for Out of Home media.

4   Measuring radio audiences

Early history

> Will anyone hearing this broadcast please communicate with us, as we are anxious to know how far the broadcast is reaching and how it is being received.[1]
>
> Announcement broadcast by the first US radio station, KDKA, on its inaugural night

Just over $37 billion was spent on radio advertising in 2008, representing 7.8% of total major media expenditure worldwide.[2] Radio's share has changed little over the past few years. It also stood at 7.8% in 1999, peaking at 9.0% in 2000. Its share is expected to decline gradually over the next few years as competition from the internet and mobile advertising heats up.

Like television, radio has seen an explosion of outlets during its relatively brief history. In the United States, for example, the number of stations more than doubled from 2,819 in 1950 to 6,519 in 1970. By 2007 the number had reached more than 11,000.[3] One estimate put the total number of radio stations broadcasting worldwide at more than 40,000.[4]

New audio distribution platforms such as the internet, DAB (Digital Audio Broadcasting), the mobile phone and digital satellite radio have vastly extended the reach of the medium, allowing advertisers to target more listening occasions, places and mindsets.

Like the print and television media, radio is now a purveyor of content – in this case audio content – rather than a single distribution device relaying programmes, news, sport and music according to a fixed schedule.

Developing out of wireless telegraphy, there is some dispute as to who exactly invented the radio medium. But the word 'radio' is said to have originally been coined by a French physicist, Edouard Branly in 1897 and turned into a noun by American adman Waldo Warren a few years later. It became a common term in the United States almost immediately (although the British continued to refer to the medium as the 'wireless' for some years).[5]

Radio first appeared on the scene in 1920, with stations in both Argentina and the United States broadcasting for the first time. The medium has developed in different ways in every country. As an illustration of the disparate paths followed it is worth taking a quick look at how it has evolved in three very different parts of the world: the United States, the UK and Japan.

The United States

In November 1920, Republican Warren G. Harding was elected as the 29th President of the United States, defeating Democrat James Cox. During the campaign, Harding had promised voters a return to 'normalcy' following the excitement and disruption of the First World War.

The results were reported in all the newspapers of the time, with little attention paid to coverage of those same elections by a tiny Pittsburgh radio station, KDKA. The broadcast, though limited in its reach, was probably to have far greater significance in the long-run than the election of President Harding. There would be no 'normalcy' after this for the American media.

From a wooden shack on the roof of the Westinghouse Company's East Pittsburgh plant, five men broadcast to an unseen audience for eighteen hours. Transmitting with a power of 100 watts on a wavelength of 360 metres, they entertained their audience with the election returns and occasional music throughout the evening from 6 pm and into the next day.

Even at this early stage, the station's operators were interested in audience research, regularly broadcasting the message quoted at the beginning of this chapter.

In 1926, the Radio Corporation of America established a network of stations, NBC, in order to provide better programming and news coverage than was within the means of smaller, local outlets. The CBS audiences network quickly set up in competition.

The medium grew very rapidly in popularity. By 1940, no fewer than four out of five US households owned a radio set. They were served by more than 800 stations and networks. Advertisers too, yet to be lured by the magic of television, flocked to the medium, spending an estimated $113 million in 1935 and $215 million in 1940.[6]

During and immediately after the Second World War the radio industry continued to grow in influence and size; advertisers spent $605 million on commercials in 1950 and more than 91% of households owned a set. Then commercial television arrived to spoil the party.

The UK

While the United States radio industry pressed forward rapidly, driven by private industry, European countries operated under tight legal controls. In the UK, for example, a licence had to be obtained if a company wanted to broadcast over the airwaves.

On 15 June 1920, Marconi's Wireless Telegraph Company was licensed to conduct an experimental broadcast featuring the Australian soprano, Dame Nellie Melba. The signal was received throughout Europe and as far west as Newfoundland.

A series of other experimental broadcasts were made by Marconi and others over the following two years. But the next important stage in British radio history occurred in October 1922, with the founding of the BBC. The original remit of the company was to establish a nationwide network of radio transmitters from which they were to provide a national broadcasting service.

The company was funded by broadcast receiving licences (as it still is today), of which just under 36,000 had been issued by the end of 1922. Two years later, when the BBC was operating twenty stations, this number had grown to over a million, which itself more than doubled again over the following two years.

On 31 December 1926, the British Broadcasting Company became the British Broadcasting Corporation, gaining control of the airwaves under the terms of a Royal Charter from the Post Office, which had previously had a statutory monopoly over the company.

No other broadcasting organisation was to receive a licence to broadcast radio in the UK until 1973 – although this did not stop people from listening to overseas stations when they so wished.

Japan

Many Asian countries also began experimental radio broadcasts during the 1920s. In Japan, private petitions for broadcasting permits were filed as early as 1921 at the Communications Ministry, which required all radio equipment to be licensed.

It was determined early on for technical and economic reasons that only one station would be licensed in each city or region. Advertising was banned, ensuring the medium's early dependence on government, rather than its own independent revenue sources. Income was to come from a combination of licence fees from listeners and taxes on radios sold.

On the editorial side, the government planned to pre-censor and monitor all programmes, warning that:

> The Japanese character and lifestyle were different from those in the West. Japan was not yet wealthy enough to accommodate a pleasure-seeking way of life and many Japanese, unlike Westerners, worked all day and well into the night, so radio entertainment should not lure them from their jobs. Radio would have to attract its audience with programming of practical value.[7]

At the end of 1923 a ministerial decree set out the prices and conditions for operating a radio licence. These have been succinctly summarised by Gregory Kasza:

> It fixed the name, call sign, transmission frequency, electric power, operating hours and cost of listeners' fees for each station. The Ministry could adjust the fees or withdraw the right to collect them. Prior-day reporting of programme content was instituted and the regional Communications Bureau Chiefs could order broadcasts in the public interest. Commercials were banned.
>
> Technical personnel had to be licensed and could be dismissed by officials. The State could command changes in broadcasting facilities, restrict or ban their use, assume direct management, or purchase all or part of them. This authority was unconditional. Station operators had to perform all obligations with their own money, including construction of new facilities at the state's behest. The approval of facilities was good for ten years, but it could be revoked in case of

non-compliance. This order too could be changed by the Ministry at any time.[8]

The first public broadcasts originated from the Tokyo Broadcasting Company in March 1925. Other stations were set up in Osaka and Nagoya. However, it wasn't long before the government decided to consolidate its control, merging all three independent broadcasting companies into a single national monopoly, Nihon Hoso Kyokai (NHK) in 1926.

Despite these restrictions, NHK succeeded in adding sixteen regions to its network on top of the original three by 1932, by which time an estimated 26% of metropolitan households and 5% of rural dwellings owned a radio. National relay programmes dominated the schedule.

By 1941, Japan's 6.6 million radio receivers put the country fourth in the world in terms of the total number of radio sets – behind the United States, Germany and the UK.

Then the Second World War intervened.

Audience measurement: a historical snapshot

Despite being off the starting block 2,000 years later than the print medium, radio audience measurement developed earlier and more quickly than it did for newspapers and magazines, with the United States setting the pace.

Because the medium was funded by advertising, the stations and networks needed to give advertisers some idea of who was listening to their commercials in order to price the airtime correctly.

Early on in its history, radio sets were large devices which sat in the home. Audience measurement was therefore to focus, as it was to do for television, on measurement of these sets and of household behaviour.

But quite quickly, the medium morphed into a more portable device. People could listen in their cars and various other locations. The challenge then became to measure people on the move.

At first, stations simply examined the number of letters sent in by listeners.[9] NBC reported receiving a million letters in 1929 and twice that many the following year.[10] But given that the kinds of people who took it upon themselves to write letters to the stations were themselves somewhat atypical, they could not be said to 'represent' listeners in any systematic way.

So in 1928 NBC commissioned Daniel Starch to conduct what today might be called an Establishment or Enumeration Survey in order to determine just how far the radio medium had penetrated American homes. 17,000 personal interviews were conducted in 105 towns and cities as well as in 68 rural counties east of the Rockies in the spring of that year.

The study found that just under 35% of the homes surveyed owned a radio, although the numbers were rising fast, making the survey out of date almost as soon as it was released.

In 1929 Archibald Crossley compiled a report for the Association of National Advertisers (ANA), *The Advertiser Looks at Radio*, which summarised results from 31,000 interviews carried out into people's radio listening.

The data produced on radio usage, the popularity of certain programmes and how audiences varied by city and time of day was well received, resulting in his company going ahead with a regular series of reports for buyers of radio time – with the endorsement of the ANA.

The new survey was conducted by telephone, covered 50 cities and asked 68,000 respondents in its first year about their listening habits on the previous day. It was to run for sixteen years.

In 1934 Clark-Hooper Inc. introduced a competitive survey. This employed what was called the 'co-incidental' method, in which respondents in sixteen cities were telephoned and asked not what they had listened to at some point in the past, but what they were listening to at the time of the call.

The study was initially funded by a group of magazine publishers as a spoiler – they felt that Crossley's numbers overstated the radio audience, helping the medium to encroach on their advertising income. As they had hoped, the first set of ratings generated by the new method were significantly lower than Crossley's for most programmes.

Despite this, Clarke-Hooper eventually managed to secure support from the radio networks. Mainly, this was because they had not been allowed to subscribe to the Crossley reports, as the ANA did not want its research to be seen as being sullied by the media. So the industry was presented with two sets of different audience estimates early on.

The Clarke-Hooper method was refined and expanded over the following years. However, a number of problems were apparent early on.

First, telephones were not universally present in American households at the time, excluding a chunk of the population. Second, many respondents were irritated at their listening being interrupted mid-flow. There was another objection to asking people what they were listening to: would they tell the interviewer what they thought they *ought* to be listening to (or not be listening to) – or what they actually listened to?

In 1942 the A.C. Nielsen company addressed this by introducing a mechanical audimeter which had been invented by academics at the Massachusetts Institute of Technology a few years previously. It was placed initially into 800 homes in the eastern United States and connected to their radio receivers.

The audimeter, which was placed unobtrusively in the household, made a taped record of the times and days when the set was in use and the stations to which it was tuned. It was an exciting development in audience measurement; indeed the forerunner of today's much more advanced meters measuring both radio and television. No longer could people tell fibs about the programmes they tuned into. Nor would it matter if they couldn't remember exactly when they had done so.

But the meters were not without their drawbacks. They often broke down (approximately 10% were said to fail each month![11]). In addition, they did not give any indication of who was listening when the radio set was switched on. Nevertheless, they became the gold standard of national audience ratings for the next few years, expanding to cover most of the country by 1949.

Three problems arrived in the 1950s to challenge both radio's dominance and its audience measurement methods: the arrival of television, the growth of in-car listening and the spread of portable radios. Listening outside the home was clearly increasing in importance, yet could not be captured by the now-dominant audimeter.

It was increasingly important that whatever measurement radio had should be at least as good, in advertisers' minds, as the television ratings now being conducted by Nielsen. In particular, they needed to be able to measure out-of-home listening.

By the 1960s it was clear that neither the Hooper nor the Nielsen audimeter services were up to the task and both services fizzled out. Nielsen shut down its audimeter operation in 1964. Hooper carried on for a few more years then it, too, threw in the towel.

A third service, the Sindlinger Radio Activity Service, offered national reports to the radio networks which employed daily telephone samples of individuals (rather than households) for a brief period in the early–mid 1960s, but did not achieve enough support to continue.

Of concern to the networks and agencies was the fact that none of the audience levels generated by the different services seemed to bear any relationship to each other.

What was needed was a service that was credible to all parts of the industry: networks and stations, advertisers and agencies. The solution had to measure all listening by everybody both by time of day and by station and on a cumulative basis – so advertisers could analyse campaigns over a period of time to ascertain how many of their target audience were reached by them.

Local radio stations and national networks remained distinct in both commercial and research terms, as far as advertisers and agencies were concerned. For this reason, two new services were inaugurated, eventually placing a cap on the disorder of the early 1960s and putting into place a system that lasted for more than 35 years.

The first was RADAR – Radio's All Dimension Audience Research. RADAR recruited panels of listeners and polled them by telephone every day for a week, asking about listening behaviour on the previous day – thus creating in effect a 'diary' of listening by network and by quarter hour, enabling campaign reach and frequency analyses to be carried out by agencies.

It also cross-tabulated this information with network radio 'clearance' information (i.e. a record of the times and days on which radio stations aired network programming) so that audiences to network commercials could be estimated. RADAR's first report appeared in 1967.

The second service was Arbitron's seven-day diary, with respondents recruited by telephone, measuring audiences to local radio. This was also launched in 1967.

Radio being more of a personal medium meant that a diary needed to be kept by each person over 12 years of age in a selected household, as their listening habits were likely to differ substantially from each other. But diaries were not a new media measurement technique.

The first use of a diary to record radio listening occurred in April 1934, when NBC included a space for it in an 'activity' diary placed with 3,042 housewives nationwide.[12]

A number of other radio networks, including CBS, experimented with diaries in the 1940s, while Nielsen's US local television measurement service, launched in the nation's 30 largest cities in 1955, used diaries in conjunction with meters attached to the television set.

These diaries had also included measurement of local radio at first, although the radio part was discontinued in 1963. But the fact that television was being measured in this way helped to provide the diary method with legitimacy in the marketplace.

Diaries continue (outside the largest cities) to be the most widely used source of audience data for both local television and local radio in the United States.

Radio audience measurement worldwide

Around 76 countries worldwide carry out radio audience measurement surveys of one sort or another – some using more than one method for various reasons. These break down into those where diary measurement is employed (29 countries), electronic measurement (12 countries), telephone day-after-recall (18 countries) and face-to-face interviews – generally as part of multi-media surveys (21 countries) – see Table 4.1.

Diaries vs. recall

The main advantage of a diary is that it facilitates the measurement of people's listening behaviour over time. This allows advertisers to examine how many of a given group of individuals will hear one or more of their commercials over the course of a campaign, rather than simply counting those who might hear individual spots.

Critics of the diary method point out that many respondents may not complete their diary systematically as they should. Instead, they might wait until the end of the week, before either the interviewer arrives to collect it or they need to send it back, and then fill in whatever they can remember for the previous week's listening. This leads to them remembering the significant and regular listening events and forgetting more incidental and irregular listening.

There could also be errors if respondents fill in their diaries either ahead of time or afterwards with a record of what they 'usually' listen to rather than what they actually listened to that week. Smaller, less habitual

Table 4.1 Radio measurement methods, March 2009

Region	Diary	Telephone DAR	Face-to-face recall	Electronic
Europe	Belgium, Estonia, Finland, Hungary, Latvia, Lithuania, Macedonia, Netherlands, Poland, Romania, Russia, Serbia, Slovakia, Sweden, Turkey, UK	Austria, Bosnia-Herzegovina, Croatia, France, Germany, Italy, Luxembourg, Portugal, Spain, Sweden	Czech Republic, Greece, Ireland, Switzerland	Belgium (Flemish region), Cyprus, Denmark, Iceland, Liechtenstein, Norway, Switzerland
North America	United States, Canada	–	–	USA, Canada (Quebec and Montreal)
South America	–	Argentina, Brazil, Mexico, Venezuela±	Bolivia, Chile, Colombia, Costa Rica, Guatemala, Peru, Uruguay, Venezuela*	–
Middle East and Africa	South Africa	Egypt, Kuwait, Lebanon, Saudi Arabia, UAE	Bahrain, Iraq, Jordan, Oman, Qatar, Syria	Kenya
Asia Pacific	Australia, China, India, Indonesia, Japan, Malaysia, New Zealand, the Philippines, Thailand, Vietnam	–	Taiwan, Hong Kong, South Korea	Kazakhstan, Singapore

*Venezuela expected to launch in 2009 (EGM survey)
±Measures car radio listening by mobile phone

Notes:
1. Each method (e.g. 'diary') can be executed differently in every market
2. Some countries use multiple methods and so are listed more than once
3. In several markets (e.g. China, India, Indonesia, the Philippines, Thailand and Vietnam) only major cities are measured

listening occasions may be omitted. These errors are thought to benefit larger stations and more popular dayparts at the expense of smaller stations and dayparts.

On top of this, the task being asked of respondents has become increasingly difficult as the number of station choices has grown. They are asked to record, quarter hour by quarter hour, any listening to any radio station, usually for at least seven days. Yet there are hundreds – if not thousands – of listening options available to people in the developed world. Not only do they have a large number of local and national stations broadcasting in their own areas, but also the internet offers free and easy access to many more from outside their region or country.

Diaries have evolved to cope with this increased complexity. For example in the UK, the RAJAR (RAdio Joint Audience Research) diary begins with a face-to-face interview at the stage when respondents are recruited. During this interview, demographic information is collected, as well as claimed access to the main digital platforms.

At the same time, a card sort procedure is completed to generate what are known as 'personal station repertoires', which determine the stations to be included in the diary. This is in some ways akin to the 'screening' procedure that occurs at the beginning of many readership surveys.

Every diary, in other words, is individual to that respondent. They do not have to look through long lists of stations or try to remember the call sign every time they listen so it can be noted in the diary.

As with most other diary services around the world, respondents are subsequently asked to record all their listening for periods of five minutes or more in any quarter hour period to these and any other stations (which can still be added in if required) during the following survey week.

They should include all stations and listening occasions, irrespective of the platform where they hear them (radio content can be accessed via digital televisions, on the internet, or via mobile devices, as well as from analogue and digital radio sets). RAJAR diaries are collected personally by interviewers and returned for processing. The published results show the stations tuned, the times at which listening takes place, the platforms where the signal is heard and the locations of that listening.

Another more general issue facing research companies which operate diary surveys is the general decline in response rates to any kinds of interview. Response rates can be particularly challenging to maintain for this kind of market research, which involves continuous commitment by the respondent over seven days.

The emergence of new electronic devices capable of more passive monitoring of television viewing and radio listening has been used to give backing to some of these criticisms by showing very different results to those produced by the diaries. At the same time, the number of viewing and listening options has continued to mushroom, compounding the problems of response and co-operation.

The Day After Recall technique has the advantage that it is asking people about something that happened a very short time ago, making it more likely they will remember it. The fact that they are speaking to an interviewer also means that they cannot leave the remembering until the last minute – they must do it then and there.

Another advantage is that very large samples can deliver information rapidly for less than the cost of administering a diary survey. In a comparison between the telephone recall and diary approaches carried out with matched samples in France,[13] it was found that overall listening patterns were similar between the two methods though, as in other such comparative studies, diarists recorded higher listening claims than people asked to remember their radio listening on the previous day.

Critics of the recall approach point out that memory is always imperfect, even on the following day, so they might easily forget non-usual listening behaviour. A study in Canada,[14] for example, found that around a fifth of people often didn't actually know what radio station they were listening to – a problem for the telephone recall method.

Diary keepers are supposed, of course, to record listening as it happens or shortly afterwards. Although it is difficult to establish the truth of this one way or the other, a 1992 research study by BBM in Canada, covering 350 diary respondents, did suggest that about one-quarter of individuals surveyed completed their radio diary in 'real time'. Another 57% completed their radio diary daily. In all, therefore, the study reported that 82% of respondents did at least claim to have noted their listening behaviour every day. Even for those who didn't, it is not unreasonable to believe that the very fact they were being asked to complete a diary would improve listening recall – which, say the adherents of the recall method, is why diary audiences are usually reported as higher than their approach – respondents are being conditioned to listen in non-normal ways.

But by establishing either a personal station repertoire or other place where stations can be listed on the diary, a continuous prompt of the various station names is available which may help people to identify what they have been listening to better than when they are cold-called.

Finally, the diary leaves a paper trail – it is possible to look back at what respondents actually said about their radio listening. This is less easy with a telephone interview (although interviews can be recorded). But the onus on a high quality of interviewing is considerable, given the kinds of confusion people may have when asked to recall their listening behaviour.

The All Radio Methodology Study

One of the earliest – and most expensive – pieces of methodological research carried out into the measurement of radio listening was the All Radio Methodology Study (ARMS) in the United States.

The 1965 study began by establishing benchmarks or what were called 'standards' for actual radio listening at home and in cars through a combination of telephone co-incidental interviews (i.e. 'what are you listening to now'), in-car meters and street intersection interviews. This was considered to be as close to true listening as could be achieved at the time.

Eleven methods were used to measure listening in Philadelphia, with samples of roughly 1,000 for each approach. Results were then compared with the standards. Diaries of various kinds made up five of the techniques. It was found that radio was best measured without other media and that personally placed and picked-up diaries had the closest fit with the standards – i.e. were the most accurate of the alternatives then available.

But response rates and co-operation were high in the early 1960s. Just over 5,000 radio stations were broadcasting. Another US study in 1974–75[15] found that households filling in diaries measuring television viewing tended to watch more television overall than non-responders and that there were considerable errors in diary filling.

Since then, response rates to market research have plummeted and the number of stations has grown. There are now around 11,000 radio stations broadcasting in the USA and radio can be listened to in the home, in the car, through PCs, TVs and via iPods.

Work has been carried out in other markets in order to try to determine whether to use a recall or a diary technique to measure radio audiences.

In India, for example, the Media Research Users Committee (MRUC) carried out a pilot study in 2007 to compare the two methods, concluding that diary-measured audiences were higher and less accurate than the recall approach.

To assess the problem of respondents not filling in their diaries in a timely manner, some diaries were collected daily and others weekly.

A face-to-face co-incidental check was made on a sample of people to establish 'true' listening levels (i.e. at the time of the visit).

Diaries collected weekly were found to be less accurate than those collected daily. But neither corresponded with the recall data. As an example, at the time of the co-incidental check where people were found not to be listening to radio, the diary reported twice as many instances of listening as the recall method.[16] The finding that diary audiences tended to be higher was consistent with European data.[17]

Ironically, the industry has ended up using the diary method to measure listening in India's major cities.

New challenges

Telephone has traditionally been the primary means of recruiting either diary or recall respondents. A growing issue for this approach is that more and more households in advanced industrial economies are giving up their landlines in favour of mobile phones. These kinds of household tend to be different in demographic and – in the United States – in ethnic composition.

Laws on privacy in many countries make it difficult, if not impossible, to randomly call mobile phone numbers for recruitment purposes.

Electronic measurement of radio audiences

Recently, radio has been the battleground of a new approach to audience measurement, not entirely unlike that experienced by the television industry in the 1980s, when it moved from a part diary/recall approach to an electronic system. As yet, there are no signs that this battle for the radio audience measurement crown has been won.[18]

Nevertheless, Passive, Portable and Personal have become the buzzwords in radio audience measurement. Several devices have been developed. The main five are:

- *Arbitron's Portable Peoplemeter (PPM).* PPMs measure listening through a small pager-like device carried by respondents throughout the day, which picks up specially encoded signals transmitted by participating stations. The system works by inserting an inaudible code into a broadcast transmission at the radio station.

It is currently the most developed of the five electronic techniques listed here. Arbitron has rolled out the system as the radio buying 'currency' in fifteen US cities (as at March 2009) as well as in key markets in Canada. They have also been deployed in Belgium, Denmark, Iceland, Kenya, Kazakhstan, Norway and Singapore, while the meter has been tested in several other countries.[19]

- *GfK Eurisko's Media Monitor*. An 'audio matching' pager-type device developed in Italy. The device samples the sounds to which the respondents are exposed. A central monitoring station records the broadcasts of all relevant radio stations and compares them with the samples in the media monitor device. Special buttons can collect additional information such as location of respondent and active or passive listening.

The device was used to collect data in a large-scale Italian multi-media study piloted in 2006 and 2007 (described more fully in Chapter 8), but which began fieldwork in February 2009. Results were not available at the time of writing.

- *GfK/Telecontrol's MediaWatch* also uses audio-matching techniques. A microphone is built into a wristwatch which records, compresses and stores snippets of sound received from the wearer's exposure to radio (or other audio content, for example, from television). This can be done up to six times every minute if required, with each snippet lasting 4 seconds. As with the Eurisko meter, radio programmes are recorded at central locations and stored in the same proprietary format used by the MediaWatch.

The two audio streams are then compared and matched, allowing each respondent's listening behaviour to be reconstructed. It is also possible for the device to identify the listening platform through the use of encoding on a selective basis if required.

A key advantage toted for the system is that it requires very little effort on the part of the respondent, who merely has to wear it as an ordinary wristwatch (it also tells the time).

The device has been used to measure radio listening in Switzerland since the beginning of 2001 and in Cyprus since 2006 as the industry currency. However, results of a series of laboratory tests carried out in the UK by RAJAR on its ability to accurately measure radio listening in various environments were not favourable – although proponents of the MediaWatch claim that, in the test, people did not wear the watches in a 'normal' way. The device identified fewer listening occasions than other methods.

- *The IMMI Phone Meter* captures listening using a mobile phone. Like the WatchMeter, it is considered to be less burdensome – i.e. more normal – for respondents to carry around with them than it is for them to carry a special meter.

  IMMI's embedded mobile phone software records 10 seconds of audio every 30 seconds and codes it into digital signatures for further analysis. In other words, unlike the PPM, its passive digital monitoring requires no input from the advertiser or content distributor. This also means that exposure to specific commercials can be picked up and identified by the system.

  An added feature of the system is that it can tell whether the respondent is in or out of the home using the mobile phone's Bluetooth technology.

  A limited technical trial of the IMMI Phone Meter was conducted in Australia with Nielsen Media Research, although little has been heard of the meter with respect to the radio audience measurement business since the trial was announced in 2008.

- *Ipsos MediaCT's MediaCell*, like the IMMI Phone Meter, also uses a mobile phone to collect listening data. It does, however, require radio stations to encode their broadcasts. As of mid-2009, the meter was still undergoing technical trials.

All five of the electronic devices described here offer the potential for a more comprehensive and detailed picture of the stations to which people are exposed (or, as critics have suggested, who are 'in the vicinity of a radio signal' – which may not be the same thing as 'listening').

All make no demands on the respondent's memory – excepting the need for them to carry the device at all times and to remember to charge it. The fundamental differences between them include the type of device (embedded in a mobile phone or watch or a special meter) and whether or not a special code needs to be embedded into the broadcast.

Early tests carried out by Arbitron on its Portable Peoplemeters in the cities of Philadelphia and Houston showed, first, that overall audience patterns were quite close to those recorded using the diary method. But while cumulative audiences were higher, average quarter-hour audiences were lower.

The results also showed that people listened to more stations, on more occasions and for shorter periods than the diaries had previously reported.[20]

Prime time listening levels are lower on the PPM than they were using the diary, while non-prime time listening is greater. Smaller stations have gained some share versus their bigger competitors.

A side-by-side test between the diary and Eurisko Media Monitor was carried out in Belgium in 2006. Unfortunately, much of the meter data was lost due to operational difficulties, meaning the usable samples were quite low.

However comparing data recorded by a diary and the meter from the same set of people at the same time, it was found that average audiences were almost halved when comparing the meter results with the diary.[21] The industry there did not feel the time was yet right to introduce meters as an audience trading currency for radio.

A number of concerns have been raised about the accuracy and validity of the PPMs (which may apply to other forms of electronic measurement, once more experience has been gained in their use). For example:

- *Compliance.* PPM carriers need to keep their device with them at all times in order to successfully simulate their radio listening. Evidence from the United States is that compliance has varied across different demographic groups. In particular, it has been found that ethnic minorities have been less compliant than other demographic groups which, in turn, has led to lower listening claims being reported for these groups. This has caused a furious debate in the industry and even prompted legal challenges from stations that rely on these groups for their audience – and advertising revenue.

- *Early morning listening.* Mornings have traditionally been primetime for radio listening, with the highest recorded audiences. Insofar as people are hurrying to prepare for work or school, possibly not fully dressed and focused on many activities, they may be less likely to remember to carry their PPMs with them than at other times of day. It is the most important time of day to measure accurately for the medium.

- *Cost.* The PPM is far more expensive to implement than non-electronic methods to which the industry has become accustomed.

In the world of radio audience measurement diaries remain in the ascendant, partly due to cost considerations, but also because questions remain over the newer passive techniques. The power of inertia must never be under-estimated either. The fact that there will be winners and losers if any large-scale changes are made leads naturally to vetoes being put on any change until it is absolutely certain that it is the right way to proceed.

Radio engagement studies

Ever since the rise of commercial television in the 1950s, radio has been seen as a secondary, background medium; an accompaniment to other activities like driving, working or reading.

As a consequence, many marketers feel it lacks the intrusiveness of television or the communications ability of print or the internet.

Yet radio can play to a number of important strengths as an advertising medium, evidence for which has been assembled by organisations such as the Radio Advertising Bureaux in various countries[22] and the Radio Effectiveness Lab (RAEL, now RAL) in the United States. These include its:

- ability to target narrowly;
- role as a 'theatre of the mind' (i.e. listeners build their own visual images as they listen);
- ability to complement other media like television (e.g. through 'visual transfer')
- mobility (i.e. listening via car radios, mobile phones, podcasting and laptop computers);
- interactivity (ability for listeners to talk back via letter/telephone/email/text);
- non-intrusiveness (strength as background medium).

Many marketers assess and track the effectiveness of their advertising through measuring whether people are aware of it and whether the particular messages are getting through. But consumers in advertising-recall studies often have great difficulty telling researchers *where* they have been exposed to advertising, attributing messages to television even if they have not actually run in the medium.

A second way in which advertising effectiveness is measured is through market mix modelling. But market mix models frequently fail to register any effects from radio advertising either because campaign weights are low in relation to other media or because no continuous audience measurement is available.

As we transition to a world of digital media, accountable advertising investment and 'holistic' marketing solutions, what case can the radio medium build for staying on the schedule?

US studies in the 1960s and 1970s revealed that radio listeners were, unsurprisingly, not paying full attention to the radio for the whole time they were within earshot of its signal. Just how much attention was being paid, according to the respondents' own definition, varied considerably between studies although, as a rule of thumb, about one third of total listening time seemed to be composed of 'fully attentive' listening.[23]

Listening in the car or at home tended to be more intense than listening at work. Other variables included time of day, the type of station and exactly what was airing (whether advertising or programming). The degree of advertising clutter also has an impact on listening, as it does on television viewing, whether it causes people to switch stations or simply to tune out – although few studies exist that quantify this behaviour.

A summary of 50 radio research studies from around the world pulled together by the RAEL in 2002[24] concluded that:

- *Radio advertising is remembered* – as instanced by at least 40 of the studies looked at. RAEL cites as one example a telephone recall study in Quebec, Canada[25] where respondents exposed to 36 radio-only advertising campaigns were able to name the advertised brands 2.5 times more frequently than those not exposed.

  The study also showed that recall tended to grow by 4 points for every 100 GRPs delivered over a three-week period up to a ceiling of 900 ratings, where incremental recall-build levelled off.

- *Radio advertising recall is about 80% of television recall.* 25 of the RAEL-listed studies included some comparative data on television and radio. The 80% estimate is based on a single exposure to an ad. Example studies cited included one carried out in Norway[26] in 1999, where a comparison of 9 radio-only and 12 radio/television campaigns concluded that radio had about 61% of the television recall level. Another from Canada[27] in 1997 found aided recall of radio advertising to be 83% that of television.

- *Radio ads vary widely in effectiveness.* RAEL cites about 20 studies where 'meaningful differences' were found between the best and worst ads. In particular, the best radio and the best television advertising tended to be much closer in impact than the two media in general[28] (suggesting less attention is paid to making great radio commercials than to getting it right on television). Some fairly dated US work concluded that 30-second ads delivered about 85% of the 'proven recall' of a 60-second ad; also that hammering home the brand name as many times as possible seemed to help people remember the brand better.
- *Radio ads produce recall even with distraction.* Classic studies such as the UK Ironing Board[29] and Jigsaw[30] studies attempted to put respondents into situations where radio was playing in the background while they focused on everyday tasks. The former found that 25% of participants could spontaneously recall some aspect of the ads playing.

Work in several countries has explored the idea that some of the power and influence of television can be transferred over to radio through a mechanism known as 'visual transfer'. A study, again in Canada[31] in 1997, found that three-quarters of people to whom a radio ad was played could conjure up an image of a matching television ad. This followed research in the UK[32] and the USA[33] with almost identical findings.

Another key argument used to market radio is as a complement to television, rather than an alternative. Radio stations realise that it is far easier to try to persuade advertisers to shift some of their money from television into radio than to move all of it. Three core arguments are offered in favour of a combined radio/television strategy:

- *The ability to build cost-effective reach.* Plenty of studies have demonstrated that radio can add reach to a television campaign, getting the message to new people at a lower cost than trying to reach them with additional TV activity.[34]
- *Visual transfer.* Impactful television advertising can be brought to mind by hearing a soundtrack, transferring the visual power of the television advertising to radio (see above).
- *Message magnification.*[35] Messages seen or heard from multiple sources can re-enforce and augment each other.

A further piece of work by RAEL in 2004 demonstrated that shifting money between television and radio (i.e. running one TV and two radio ads in place of running just two TV ads) generated 34% higher unaided brand recall, 15% higher prompted recall and a 60% improvement in brand preference.[36]

German research carried out in the 1990s showed similar improvements in mixed versus single media campaigns[37] while the UK Radio Advertising Bureau's Radio Multiplier Study found that moving 10% of a television budget to radio could generate a 15% boost in awareness.[38]

Other radio research

Quite apart from general arguments as to radio's impact, there are factors within the control of the medium and the advertiser which influence the extent to which an audience engages with an ad.

Clearly the creative message itself is one of the most important of these.[39] But others such as the length of the spot, the length of the advertising break as a whole and the position the ad occupies in the break will have an impact.

Unsurprisingly, longer ad breaks with more spots tend to be inferior environments for individual commercials, while the first spot in a break generally gets noticed more. These results are similar to those found for television. The impact of spot length seems to have less effect on advertising awareness than it does on brand awareness.[40]

The future

Like other media, radio is going digital. In the USA, one consequence of this has been the growth of advertising-free, satellite-delivered services which are beginning to make inroads into the market. But it also means more stations and better signal quality for listeners generally.

For marketers and research professionals it means more audience fragmentation and greater difficulty in measuring who is listening to what. The most popular form of measurement worldwide remains the radio diary, in which respondents are asked to keep a detailed record of what they are listening to by quarter or half hour. This is a difficult task at the best of times and has become far more complex with the growth in listener choice.

It was concluded by the Research Director of the UK's RAJAR that, after testing electronic meters over an extended period of time they, like diaries, were potentially a very reliable way of collecting information on radio listening. The weakness of both methods (and, indeed, in most others) lay in the behaviour of respondents.

In his own words,[41] discussing the results of the electronic meter tests: 'Ultimately, we had to concede that the methodology was measuring people's interaction with the methodology itself, and not with the media we were supposed to be measuring.'

So radio audience measurement remains a work in progress. The challenge for the medium – as it is for all media – is to find ways to better connect its audience measures to the numbers that matter to marketers (i.e. sales, market share and profits) as everything around it changes.

5 Measuring television audiences

Introduction

> Television? The word is half Greek and half Latin. No good will come of this device.
>
> C.P. Scott, editor, *Manchester Guardian*, 1936

Not long after its first appearance in the 1930s, television was to become the dominant mass medium in the minds of most major marketers and the principal leisure activity for most consumers, first in the United States and then worldwide.

It still held first place for many of them in 2008. According to ZenithOptimedia, more than $183 billion was spent by advertisers in the medium that year,[1] representing a 38% share of major media advertising expenditure globally. ZenithOptimedia does not expect to see this share change very much over the next few years which, given the rapid rise of internet and mobile advertising, is no mean achievement.

Television is often the first communications channel a mass marketer thinks of when planning to launch a new brand or support an existing one. It offers impact through sound, pictures and motion, the ability to reach lots of people quickly and 'talkability'. No less important for many marketers, it is an important competitive battleground. If other marketers are using it, goes the reasoning, then it is important that they do too.

Research into the television audience focuses on both the rational and emotional benefits it can offer to advertisers. These include:

- How many and what kinds of people watch each programme and/ or commercial?
- What are the effects of programme and advertising *context* on attention to and response to the advertising?

- What factors might lead people to actively avoid watching advertising – either by fast-forwarding, switching channels or simply leaving the room?

Like other media, television faces enormous challenges from the growth in consumer choice and also in the enhanced ability of its audience to take control of their viewing environment.

Choice has been increased via the appearance of hundreds of new television channels, often delivered by satellite or cable. It has also mushroomed with the arrival of new ways of accessing and viewing video content.

Early history of television

Television has its earliest origins in the 1870s. It began with a chance discovery by the English electrical engineer Willoughby Smith in 1873, who had observed photoconductivity in the element selenium.

From this observation, various scientists and engineers were able to make the leap to the idea of transmitting moving pictures over the airwaves using several different approaches. By the 1920s, they were ready to start showing off their inventions publicly.[2]

On 2 November 1936 the world's first regular television service in 'high definition'* (defined as 405 lines per picture) was inaugurated by the BBC in Britain. The service was broadcast from the corporation's studios at Alexandra Palace in London, using a specially built mast on the roof of the building.

Initially, two blocks of programmes were broadcast every day except Sunday, between 15:00 and 16:00 and from 21:00 to 22:00. The service was eventually on-air an average of four hours daily from 1936 to 1939, going out to approximately 12,000–15,000 receivers.

The limited broadcasts were packed with unmissable programmes such as a *Laundry Demonstration* (ironing), *Vivienne Brooks and the Television Orchestra* and *Movietone Magic Carpets*.

Over the next three years regular electronic television broadcasts also kicked off in Germany, France, the Soviet Union and Italy.

---

* The caveat 'high definition' is important, as Germany had begun a broadcasting service using a much lower quality picture (180 lines) in March 1935.

While these developments were occurring in Europe, the United States, too, was a hive of activity. They were somewhat late to the television party owing to a protracted legal battle between Radio Corporation of America (RCA) and the inventor, Philo Farnsworth. RCA made a good deal of money from its control of radio broadcasting patents, having purchased those of Marconi and other radio pioneers. They had wanted to buy Farnsworth's television patents along with his company, but could not agree on price. RCA then decided to try and squeeze the patents out of him through the courts. First they challenged the patents then, when they lost, took the battle to the Appeal Court. The dispute dragged on, costing Farnsworth time and money he could ill afford and effectively preventing television broadcasts from starting.

However, long before the case was finally settled in 1939, RCA, knowing they would eventually prevail one way or the other, had begun to develop reliable television broadcast technology and were ready to start manufacturing receivers immediately.

The corporation's broadcasting wing, NBC, began regular television transmissions on 30 April 1939, with a broadcast of President Franklin D. Roosevelt opening New York's World Fair. The broadcast was transmitted by NBC's local station W2XBS Channel 1 and seen by about 1,000 viewers within the station's roughly 40-mile (64 km) coverage area from their Empire State Building transmitter location.

Table 5.1 gives details of first broadcasts for various countries.

The arrival of commercial television

US television's long experimental period finally ended when the Federal Communications Commission authorised full commercial broadcasting to start up on 1 July 1941.

On that date, W2XBS aired the world's first television commercial – for Bulova Watches – just prior to a baseball game between the Brooklyn Dodgers and Philadelphia Phillies. The 10-second spot showed a picture of a clock superimposed on a map of the United States, accompanied by the voice-over: 'America runs on Bulova time'.

Japan drew heavily on the US television model and also permitted commercials early on in the medium's development. However, the broadcasting scene was dominated by national broadcaster NHK, which did not accept commercials. NHK launched its service in February 1953,

Table 5.1 Launch years for television broadcasts[1] by selected country

Country	First regular television broadcast	First commercial television broadcast
United Kingdom	1936	1955
Germany	1937	1956
France	1937	1968
United States	1939	1941
Italy	1939	1957
Japan	1953	1953
Australia	1956	1956
China	1958	1979
India	1959	1967

1. Excludes 'mechanical' broadcasting, which sometimes preceded electronic broadcasts and experimental broadcasts, which sometimes continued for many years
2. A low-resolution service was launched in 1935

23 years after it had started experimental transmissions. Six months later, on 28 August, commercial station Nippon TV Network Corporation went on air.

Independent Television (ITV), funded by commercials, was launched in London on 22 September 1955, where the 'mixed model' of public and private broadcasters operating side by side was also to prevail. Commercial television was tightly regulated in the UK. The country was divided into regions, with separate contractors bidding to serve each area. Every ten years, the companies were to be reviewed to ensure they had fulfilled the terms of their licences. Amongst these conditions was an insistence that certain local television services including news were provided for their particular region.

Other countries in Europe put into place even stricter regulation of advertising in the early days. In Germany, for example, commercials were first permitted in 1956. But they were limited to 20 minutes a day, divided into a series of advertising 'blocks'. No advertising was permitted after 8.00 pm or at any time on Sundays or public holidays. And it was certainly not allowed to interrupt programmes. The system was to last for almost 30 years.

In France, the government owned and operated the broadcasting industry until 1982. Advertising was introduced in 1968, but it was heavily restricted and not expected to provide more than a quarter of overall broadcasting revenues (the rest to be made up by licence fees and state subsidies).

In Italy, it was also the intention of the government to regulate broadcasting closely. They were successful at first, although things were to fall apart in the 1970s. The medium came under the auspices of state-owned and run RAI, backed by licence fee income and supplemented by advertising from 1957.

China's first television commercial was shown in March 1979 on Shanghai Television, during live transmission of a women's basketball game. A local brand, Xingfu Cola, featured. It was a particularly significant event for this country, only just coming out of the lean years of the Cultural Revolution and into 30 years of headlong economic growth.

Colour transmissions

The first regular colour broadcasts in Europe were shown by BBC2 in the UK on 1 July 1967. West Germany and France also inaugurated colour in the same year. Norway, Sweden, Finland, Belgium, the Netherlands, Austria, East Germany, Czechoslovakia and Hungary had all transitioned to regular colour broadcasts before the end of 1969.

But Europe trailed the United States, where it had been introduced relatively early on (NBC's broadcast of *The Tournament of Roses Parade* in January 1954 was the first). Broadcasting in colour was standard there by the mid-1960s, though by 1965 only 7% of households could receive their signal on colour sets.

The number of colour television sets sold in the USA did not exceed black and white sales until 1972, also the first year that more than 50% of television households owned a colour set.

Japan was also early to colour, with broadcasts appearing from September 1960. But other countries in Asia were slower off the mark. It was introduced in China for example only in 1973, when an estimated 114 sets were in use.[3] It finally arrived in India in 1982.

Expansion of commercial broadcasting

In the United States, the medium took off almost immediately. From 4 million households at the beginning of the 1950s it expanded rapidly, reaching almost 90% of homes by 1960 and enjoying, for all intents and purposes, universal coverage from the mid-1960s. Most viewers could choose between the three national networks, NBC, CBS and ABC and, in major cities, from a handful of independent local stations.

During the 1970s, the number of independent stations expanded quickly, increasing choice in most of the big cities. By 1970 the average home could receive seven channels.

Cable television was to help boost this number considerably. It had first been introduced in the mountains of Pennsylvania to help households suffering from poor reception to improve their signal. In 1948, residents of a coal-mining town, Mahanoy City, had experienced problems getting good pictures due to the region's surrounding mountains. John Walson, who owned an appliance store in the town, had found it difficult to sell his television sets when he couldn't show people how good the picture on the sets would be. So he went out and erected an antenna on a utility pole on top of one of the mountains. He then connected the mountain antenna to his appliance store using a cable and modified signal boosters. This solved his problem. But he also helped out some of his customers with their reception problems, connecting up several of them who happened to be located along the cable path. This was the nation's first cable television system.

In 1980 a fifth of the country received their signals through cable and the average household could receive 10 channels. By 2000, three quarters received their signals other than by terrestrial means and the average household could tune into 72 channels.

In Europe, things did not move quite so fast. Governments were slow to take their hands off the controls, arguing that quality would suffer if the services were placed entirely in the hands of commercial interests.

In the UK, for example, it wasn't until 1982 that a second national commercial network, Channel 4, was licensed to begin broadcasting, breaking the 27-year commercial monopoly enjoyed by ITV.

Less than ten years later Sky Television launched a satellite-delivered service direct to UK homes. After a slow start, satellite television gradually made inroads into UK households, as Sky (renamed BSkyB) snapped up broadcasting rights for sports and films ahead of the terrestrial broadcasters. By early 2009, more than a third of the country had signed up to BSkyB's service.

Digital terrestrial television also brought more channels into viewers' homes for the price of a set-top box – without the need to pay monthly subscription fees. This, together with cable in a handful of cities, and BSkyB's satellite service put multi-channel television (anything between 25 and 400 channels, depending on the service) into almost 90% of UK homes by early 2009.

In Germany it had long been clear that allowing advertisers just 20 minutes a day was causing a great deal of pent-up demand to be created. Spurred by the rapid development of the Deutsche Bundespost's national cable network during the 1970s and 1980s and by the launch of satellites to deliver programming via this network, private broadcasters finally started to gather momentum in the late 1980s, dislodging the old order.

France began to liberalise its television broadcasting regime in 1984, beginning with the launch of Pay-TV network Canal Plus and followed two years later by the introduction of two new commercial networks and the privatisation of leading state channel TF1. By 1991, the combined share of private channels reached 60%.[4]

In Italy, the state-owned RAI channels were struggling with bureaucracy and political infighting by the 1970s. RAI's monopoly over national broadcasting had been confirmed by Law 103, passed in 1975. But the following year, the Constitutional Court ruled that it did not extend to the local level, spurring several hundred stations to set up in towns and cities. Although it was illegal for any of them to broadcast nationally, entrepreneurs like Silvio Berlusconi cleverly circumvented this law by transporting video tapes to stations around the country and broadcasting them simultaneously – giving the appearance to viewers and advertisers of being a national network. Between 1977 and 1980, he created a nation-wide network, Canale 5, using precisely this strategy. Programming was racier and more populist than RAI's, relying heavily on imported films and home-produced game shows. By 1981, the Constitutional Court decided to revise its earlier decision and ruled in favour of national private networks. Berlusconi bought out a close competitor, Italia 1, in 1982, and acquired his only other serious challenger, Rete 4, in 1984. Cable and satellite have not made the inroads into Italy that they have in other countries.

The modern television industry

The history of television around the world has taken different courses. But the outcome has been similar: as the years have passed, governments and regulators have relaxed their grip, more channels have been made available to viewers, programming has been extended around the clock and signal quality is better than it has ever been.

Many households now have hundreds of television channels available to them through a satellite or cable link. Most have several sets around their homes and the means to record and play back television programmes.

And a lot of them use the television set for other purposes such as playing video games, watching pre-recorded content or listening to the radio. Broadband internet connections now give them access to yet more content via 'catch-up' television, video download sites or video streaming.

Yet despite all these developments, the amount of time people spend watching television on their television sets has continued to grow. An analysis of viewing data from 50 countries, for example, showed that average viewing time per individual across these territories rose from 3 hours 31 minutes in 2000 to 3 hours 43 minutes in 2008.[5]

Technology has vastly extended the reach and depth of the medium, giving people seemingly endless choice and advertisers the ability to target more viewing occasions, places and mindsets. Audience measurement has developed alongside this, but certainly not at the same pace.

Audience measurement: a historical snapshot

The nature of the television medium made it a relatively easy target for audience researchers at the beginning. The television set – and therefore people's viewing – took place mainly in private households. The fact that it was in a largely fixed location meant that, once it was known which households had a set, they could be asked to take part in surveys of one sort or another.

But finding out which households owned a television was not quite so easy in the earliest days of the medium. In the United States after the Second World War for example, newspapers did not carry TV listings to the tiny number of homes that could receive signals. To ensure its viewers knew what was being broadcast therefore, NBC offered to mail its weekly schedule to anybody requesting it. Through a mail-back system, viewers had the opportunity to record which shows they had watched and any comments they might have on them.

This was the basis for the first crude television ratings in that country and, indeed, in many others. The BBC, for example, requested viewers to send in postcards in its earliest days, as did China Central Television when it started to take an interest in its audiences in the 1970s.

C.E. Hooper, who was already active in measuring radio audiences, began offering telephone-based viewing data in New York in 1947, although his focus remained very much on radio measurement. As with radio, he used what was known as the 'coincidental' technique, which involved phoning a representative sample of viewers during each half-hour of the broadcast day (which began at 5 pm) and asking whether they were watching at that moment and, if so, which programmes they were tuned to. These were then used to create audience estimates.

Because the medium was still small, with penetration unevenly distributed, a very large number of random telephone calls would normally have been necessary to locate sufficient numbers of television-owning households in the very early days. So useful assistance was given to Hooper by NBC and its parent company RCA, which were able to supply contact details of new set buyers and those who had requested TV schedule information.

In 1950 Trendex launched a service using the same approach, following the sale of Hooper's radio and national television businesses to Nielsen in that year. Reports were initially offered covering 10 cities, expanding to 27 shortly afterwards.

An alternative measurement service was offered from 1949 by the American Research Bureau (ARB). A representative sample of television households were asked to keep a record of all their television viewing for a week, indicating by quarter-hour periods in a diary when they had the set switched on, the channels they were watching and which household members were present.

Diaries offered the advantage that an entire week's viewing could be obtained from the same sample. It was also possible to see how people moved between channels and, over time, what the cumulative reach for various programmes and channels was. This was to become particularly valuable as computers began being used to analyse audience data in the 1950s and 1960s.

By 1961, ARB's service covered major local cities and markets throughout the country and also offered twice-yearly national 'sweeps' where all markets were measured at the same time.

Yet another service was launched at the same time as ARB's diary. Nielsen installed its first 'set meter' in New York to automatically record household set tuning. The device was initially placed in just over 200 households. It provided information on when the TV set was switched on and to which channel it was tuned. The information was recorded onto tapes which were mailed back to Nielsen each week.

Because the meter only provided information on set tuning, another way had to found to provide estimates of how many and what kinds of people were watching at any given time. It was initially supplemented with audience share estimates culled from Hooper's telephone studies and later, as the meter service expanded, with Nielsen's own set of household diaries, placed with a separate sample of households. The diaries reported on the numbers and the demographics of viewers (and listeners – initially, the diary measured both television and radio).

The rapid growth in the popularity of television spurred Nielsen to expand both the geographical coverage and the number of set meter households. In 1960, the company began to report national ratings based on the total number of television households – which by then had reached 90% of all homes – using a sample of 1,100 households.

Local audience measurement was provided in a growing number of individual cities based on diaries (with a local metered sample in New York from 1960 and Los Angeles from 1970).

By 1982 the national meter sample had expanded to 1,250. But by then the growth in the number of stations had began to accelerate and it was clear that the national sample would have to increase as well.

Between the 1940s and the 1970s very little happened in television audience measurement around the world that had not been tried or implemented in the United States. Telephone surveys, diaries and set meters represented the state of the art until the 1970s. Most countries that carried out any kind of audience research used one or other of these techniques. This all changed in the 1980s, with the coming of the peoplemeter.

Peoplemeters

The peoplemeter is essentially a box about the size of a paperback book with a display screen, which sits near or on top of each television set in a sample household. The meter comes with a remote control device. Each member of a household is assigned an individual button which they are asked to press every time they enter or leave a room with the television set on. All the devices in a home are connected to a central unit which is 'polled' by the research company's computer each night through the panel member's landline or mobile phone. If the TV is turned on and no viewer identifies himself, the meter flashes to remind them to press their button. Additional buttons enable guests to register their presence in the household.

The device was originally developed by UK company Audits of Great Britain (AGB) in the late 1970s and first installed in the UK and Italy in 1984. Germany and Switzerland followed in 1985 using Telecontrol meters.

The most common detection methods used were frequency-based, due to the fact that they worked by noting the frequency of each channel. Other techniques used included 'tuner' meters in which the household television and other tuners were replaced by the ones included in the peoplemeter system.

The advent of digital television, which does not support frequency measurement, has made channel identification more complex – alternatives such as audio encoding (where the broadcaster places a special code in the broadcast to identify itself) or audio matching (where snippets of sound are matched with known broadcast audio) have become widely used in recent times.

Since the early 1990s, television audiences in most countries around the world have been measured with peoplemeters. At the end of 2006 around 75 countries used electronic measurement of one sort or another, with meters installed in more than 140,000 households.[6]

The advantage of peoplemeters over diaries is, of course, that respondents need to do nothing except press their button when they start and stop viewing. They don't have to remember what they have watched, as in recall studies. They don't have to remember to fill in their diaries as they are watching. They just have to press their buttons.

Each peoplemeter service operates in a slightly different way, but broadly speaking, all will have the following characteristics:

- Some sort of 'enumeration' or 'establishment' survey will identify how many and what kinds of television household exist in all the areas that need to be measured. If there is no dedicated survey, a country's census together with data from other surveys will be used to determine how many of each type of household need to be recruited to the panel.

- The goal is to ensure that every television-owning household in a country has a known probability of being on the panel. But it is important to represent all the key variables that will affect a household's viewing. These include their location, the presence of children, the size and composition of the household, the number of channels that can be received and so on.

- Once the panel has been recruited, meters are attached to every set in the household and buttons allocated to each household member. The meters are linked to a phone line which automatically uploads the viewing information to the research company on a periodic basis. By the next morning in many markets, the ratings (known as 'overnights') are released to clients.

The United States was relatively late to the peoplemeter party in 1987. Several countries in Europe and Asia already measured television audiences using this technique – see Table 5.2. But despite being late, it now boasts by far the largest number of peoplemeter households in the world, with just under 25,000 installations (15,400 homes across 23 individual local markets and a 9,000-strong national panel). China, which launched even later, now has 15,300 installations – a 4,000-home national panel, four provincial panels totalling 2,050 homes and 44 individual city panels (including Hong Kong) totalling 9,250 homes.

Peoplemeters undoubtedly represented an improvement on the old set meter/diary panels. And they arguably provide better and more granular information on audiences to advertising than those of many other media. But, like any system for estimating audiences, they are far from perfect. Some of the weaknesses include:

- The peoplemeter universe is of necessity based on all private households (it would be impossible to install peoplemeters in hotels, bars or other public places). Viewing that takes place outside the home will not be captured.

Table 5.2 Peoplemeter launch dates and household sample sizes: selected countries

Country	Launch year	Current household sample (2008)
United Kingdom	1984	5,100
Italy	1984	5,000
Germany	1985	5,640
Switzerland	1985	1,870
Thailand	1985	1,430
Finland	1987	1,100
Netherlands	1987	1,240
Spain	1987	3,305
United States∞	1987	24,400
Belgium*	1988	1,500
Greece	1988	1,300
Canada∞	1989	4,250
France	1989	3,100
Ireland	1989	600
New Zealand	1990	500
Turkey	1990	2,000
Austria	1991	1,500
Hong Kong	1991	650
South Korea	1991	2,350
Australia	1991	6,350#
Indonesia	1991	2,273
Denmark	1992	1,020
Norway	1992	1,000
Portugal	1993	1,000
Sweden	1993	1,000
Taiwan	1993	1,800
India	1994	6,600
Japan	1994	1,800
Hungary	1994	840
Philippines	1994	1,840
Malaysia	1995	1,000
Poland	1996	1,650
Russia	1996	1,650
Czech Republic	1997	1,330
China (exc. Hong Kong)	1998	14,650
Romania	1998	1,050
Ukraine	1998	1,200
Latvia	1999	260
Slovenia	1999	450
Lithuania	2000	310
Croatia	2002	660
Serbia	2002	890
Estonia	2003	195
Slovakia	2004	800

* Launched in the southern part of Belgium first, followed by northern Belgium in 1989
# Four separate panels: metro, regional, subscription and WA
∞Includes separate national and local panels

- There is no way of knowing whether or not people press their buttons correctly every time they enter or leave the room.[7]
- Peoplemeters cannot measure attentiveness – presence in the room does not guarantee viewers are paying attention to what is on the screen.
- Sample sizes, though rising, may not be able to grow sufficiently to capture viewing across the growing number of channels available.
- Those agreeing to join a peoplemeter panel may be biased towards heavier viewers and against younger people, upper-income groups, single-person households and lighter viewers.[8] Of course this can be corrected to some extent in various ways, but the panels are unlikely to be free of this bias.[9]
- Peoplemeters measure viewing only on the television set. As other platforms such as mobile phones and the internet take a growing share of video consumption, methods will have to be devised to integrate the measurement of these platforms with the peoplemeter.

In response to some of these weaknesses, work has been going on into several devices that attempt to measure individual (rather than household) viewing and which seek to do this with minimal intervention from the respondent.

Changing the currency

As markets moved either from a diary-based measurement system or a combined diary and set meter service to peoplemeters, reported viewing figures changed, even though people's viewing habits did not.

While it might seem obvious that changing the method so fundamentally was bound to have some impact on the results (arguably – if the method was better – making the results more accurate), there were invariably going to be winners and losers in the commercial marketplace.

Television stations were suddenly faced with higher or lower audience shares than they had been used to. Programme rankings changed.

Advertisers found it especially hard to cope with changes in the measured amount they were paying to reach the television audience. They normally evaluate the costs of their investment in advertising using a benchmark known as 'cost-per-thousand' (abbreviated to CPT or, in the United States, to CPM). This is calculated using the price they pay for commercials divided by the number of people estimated to be watching them (expressed in thousands).

If a programme an advertiser had been buying into for a long period of time suddenly records a drop in reported audiences of 50% as a result of a new measurement device, the cost per thousand of his commercial slot will double, making what was once considered a good buy into a poor one.

Yet all that has really changed is the measuring device, not the actual audience. In the UK, measured audiences increased substantially when peoplemeters replaced the old set meter/diary system. Overall hours of television viewing were 14% higher in 1985, the first full year of the peoplemeter system, than they had been in 1984. And the number of programmes generating audiences of 15 million or more increased from 135 to 201.

In the United States the experience was different. There, household viewing recorded by peoplemeters was consistently *lower* than the levels recorded by the stand-alone set meters previously employed on the national sample and which continued to be used in the larger local markets.[10]

These difficulties were eventually ironed out in the countries that adopted peoplemeters, but it was often a difficult transition.

There are peoplemeters … and peoplemeters

The widespread adoption of peoplemeters did not suddenly harmonise audience measurement. As we have seen with readership measurement, there are many different ways in which a methodology can be implemented which will affect the audience estimates generated – even small differences can have an impact. Some of the important variations include:

- *Geographic coverage.* Not all meter systems cover the entire population of a country. In Japan, for example, only the three largest cities are equipped with peoplemeters; the rest are still measured by a combination of set meters and diaries. Similarly, in Russia, Ukraine, Turkey and many other countries around the world, only major urban centres are covered by the research.
- *Definition of viewing.* In some markets (e.g. the UK and France), panellists are asked to register their presence in the room. In others,

such as the United States and Italy, they are requested to press their buttons only if they are in the room *and watching*.

- *Guest viewing.* The viewing of guests in a peoplemeter home may or may not be included in the audience estimates, although it is in the majority of markets. It can make a difference of 5–8% in the total level of viewing reported.
- *VCR/PVR playback.* As discussed in detail below, although VCR playback never accounted for as much viewing as was originally thought, Personal Video Recorders (PVRs) are making increasing inroads into 'live' audiences and so, ideally, need to be included in the ratings calculation in some way.
- *Persistence levels.* This is a technical term referring to the amount of time a viewing event needs to last before the meter will register that it is taking place. So, for example, if the persistence is set at 15 seconds and a viewer switches from Channel A to Channel B for 12 seconds, then to Channel C for 9 seconds and then back to Channel A – no change in viewing will be recorded. In some countries (e.g. Austria) it is set at 30 seconds; in others (Spain, Portugal) as low as 5 seconds. 15 seconds tends to be the most common setting.
- *Reporting conventions.* The diary tended to collect and report viewing by quarter hour. The meter can collect data every second. But reporting conventions vary. For example, depending on the country, a commercial can be attributed the average audience of the minute it appears in, of the minute in which it begins, of the minute where the majority of the spot appears or even of the average audience to the entire commercial break.
- *The age range of panellists.* This can vary quite considerably between countries. For example, the minimum age at which viewers are asked to participate in the panel is 3 in France and Germany, 4 in the UK and 6 in Switzerland. In the United States it is 2!

Peoplemeters represented an important advance on the diary method. But the same factors that raised challenges for the diaries – increasing numbers of channels and falling co-operation rates – have not gone away.

A new generation of so-called 'passive' measurement devices have been tested and, in some cases, have been implemented to measure television audiences.

Passive measurement devices

The most developed of these to date has been Arbitron's Portable Peoplemeter (PPM).* In the form of a pager, the PPM is designed to be carried by respondents during their waking hours. It picks up any exposure these people have to encoded audio signals embedded in the television programmes being aired, wherever they may be.[11]

Advantages cited for the PPM and other 'passive' devices include the fact that respondents do not have to remember to press buttons when they enter and leave a room and that exposure outside of the home can be picked up.

A disadvantage is that 'presence in the vicinity of an audio signal' (the PPM definition of a television viewer) is not the same thing as actually watching the television.

Arguably, of course, 'presence in a room with the television set on' may not accurately represent the number of people actually watching television either.

But the link between attentive viewing and measured exposure to an audio signal is likely to be weaker outside the home than it is inside, with 'viewers' possibly just passing by locations which happen to have televisions switched on. This will need to be accounted for by those using the audience estimates.

Another challenge for the PPM has been to ensure that respondents actually carry their devices with them throughout the day and that they do it consistently and continuously.

But the contentious point for marketers at the end of the day is that the audience results generated by these two devices vary, often considerably, just as they did when peoplemeters replaced diaries. The problem then becomes one of deciding which of them is closer to the 'truth' or, more realistically, is commercially acceptable to all sides of the buying and selling equation.

All of the electronic devices currently being tested or used offer the potential for a more comprehensive and detailed picture of the programmes and video content to which people are exposed. They make little demand on the respondent's memory – excepting the need for them to carry the device at all times and to remember to charge it.

---

* See Chapter 4 (radio) for a full description of passive measurement devices.

Return Path Data

An increasing limitation of sample-based TV audience measurement (such as both peoplemeter and PPM panels) is the growing fragmentation of audiences.[12]

In the USA, for example, the *average* household now receives more than 100 channels. In the UK, of 250 channels measured in April 2009, only 11 achieved an audience share exceeding 1%.[13]

As a result, while niche channels may offer targeting opportunities for advertisers, their tiny ratings are often swamped by channel surfers moving up and down their Electronic Programme Guides.[14] One solution proffered has been to model individuals' viewing from large household panels.[15] This may become more popular if a method known as Return Path Data or RPD takes root.

RPD describes the use of the set-top boxes (that bring cable, satellite and other digital signals into households) to gather more detailed television tuning data.

In the United States, several projects are running including one from TNS, which takes detailed tuning behaviour from 270,000 digital subscriber households belonging to cable operator Charter in Los Angeles.[16] Nielsen and Rentrak also have access to data from Charter's Los Angeles subscribers, while Rentrak and TNS work with set-top box data from the DISH satellite network.

One of the most ambitious initiatives in the United States to date is a plan by Canoe Ventures, a company jointly owned by the nation's six largest cable operators, to integrate set-top box data from their combined 57 million set-top boxes covering 32 million households.

With Return Path Data, viewing records can be examined right down to the second-by-second level with robust data for almost any sized channel or programme.[17] If data can also be matched with product purchasing, even more interesting findings can emerge.[18]

Of great interest to advertisers will be the possibilities opened up to deploy 'addressable' advertising – i.e. to send advertisements only to households where it is thought viewers will be receptive – such as advertising to children only in households where there are children.

Return Path Data is not without its limitations. It can only record what is happening to the television set, rather than what people in front of the set are doing. There are other, more practical obstacles. For example:

- Many householders fail to switch off their box completely (leaving it in standby mode), even when the set is off and they are no longer watching. This can lead to false viewing being credited to the last channel viewed. Nielsen has estimated that some 10% of set-top boxes are not switched off from month to month.[19]
- There are many different models and types of set-top box. Not all of them can send data back and many of those that do use inconsistent data formats.
- Although the viewing information is anonymised, data privacy will be an important element of securing viewer co-operation with the system. Many households may, given the choice, refuse to have their viewing behaviour tracked.

But all this said, there is clearly potential, once these and other issues have been tackled, to find ways of integrating panel-based data on the behaviour of individuals with that of near-census data on television set usage.

New challenges

In the world of television audience measurement, peoplemeters remain in the ascendant, partly due to cost considerations, but also because questions remain over the newer passive techniques – just as they did over peoplemeters themselves when the industry began to move away from using diaries.

The fact that there will be winners and losers if any large-scale changes are made leads naturally to vetoes being put on any change until it is absolutely certain that it is the right way to proceed.

The wider challenges facing all market research also face television audience researchers: finding enough people willing to take part in long-term panels that measure their viewing. Already, market researchers are finding it increasingly difficult to contact people randomly either by knocking on their doors or by cold calling them. Security concerns have made people less willing to entertain strangers in their homes or even to let them get as far as the front door if they live in doorman-controlled apartments or gated estates. Telephone answering machines are commonly used to screen calls.

A newer concern is the growing incidence of mobile phone-only households – where people no longer have landlines. In the United States for example, an estimated 17.5% of households fell into this category in 2008, with a wide variation from state to state.[20] In Finland, only around a third of households have a fixed phone line![21]

In a large number of markets, random telephone calling is often the primary means by which peoplemeter samples are recruited in the first place. With no national mobile phone sampling frames in place – and the existence of privacy legislation in many countries preventing random calls to mobile phones – the ability to build truly random panels where every household has a theoretically equal chance of being included is being eroded.

The particular challenge for television audience researchers is not only to successfully negotiate all these obstacles, but then to get people to agree to be monitored for long periods of time – perhaps several years.

There is, finally, the issue of watching television through other channels such as the PC, mobile phone or games consoles – all of which are available to growing numbers of people.

Television engagement studies

Recall of television advertising has been declining over the past few decades. Although regular tracking of this phenomenon has not been carried out in recent years using a consistent methodology, some evidence to support it is available in a series of studies carried out for the Newspaper Advertising Bureau in the United States between 1965 and 1990.

Newspapers, of course, had every reason to want to tell the world that people did not remember television advertising. By telephoning a sample of people shortly after a commercial had aired in primetime and asking them whether they could remember which product had just been advertised, they found in their first study that about 40% of respondents either remembered the exact product and brand that had run or an earlier commercial that had been broadcast the same evening.

In the last of their studies published in 1990 the figure had fallen to 16%. In 1997, CBS fielded a similar telephone coincidental study[22] – although it was confined to Sunday evenings – finding that just 4% of respondents could, unaided, name a commercial that had run during the programmes they had been watching in the previous two hours.

Reasons for this include the substantial rise in the amount of marketing material consumers are exposed to across all media, increased awareness that they are being sold to and new technologies allowing them to avoid watching what they don't want to. As a result, much of the advertising going out over the air is not being consciously attended to by people who are officially recorded by the peoplemeters as being 'present in the room' or in the room watching television.

So the audience ratings generated by the peoplemeters and other methods are clearly a necessary – but by no means sufficient – basis for an advertiser to judge the relative value of different commercial slots. Nor can they tell a programmer everything he may wish to know about the success or otherwise of his creation.

There are two main strands of research which address the idea that some surrounding content is better than other content at focusing people's attention on a commercial, regardless of the size of that audience or the creative power of the commercial:

- Research into the *programme* environment around the advertising;
- Research into the *advertising* environment.

As will be seen, much of the work carried out on this subject defines 'effectiveness' in terms of advertising recall. Recall is not, in fact, the same thing as effectiveness, as has been confirmed by many studies.[23]

Much of the impact of advertising is implicit, in the sense that it works at a subconscious, rather than a conscious level (i.e. people may not particularly recall advertising and be able to play it back to an interviewer, but it may still be lodged in their subconscious and be played back to them when they are shopping and recognise a brand or service they have seen advertised at some point in the past).

In the absence of better data, however, recall scores remain a useful way of looking at these issues.

The programme environment

Will advertising in a programme that is closely attended to or in which viewers feel more involved have a higher impact than if the same advertising appears in a programme to which viewers pay less attention or in which they feel less involved?

The idea that high-attention programming will have an overall positive impact on the advertising has been dubbed the 'Positive Effects' Hypothesis. It is based on the argument that when people watch something they really like, they will be free of distractions and therefore more focused on what is on the screen.

Conversely, the 'Negative Effects' Hypothesis states that viewers closely involved or particularly attentive to a programme will be more irritated with commercial interruptions and more likely to seek to avoid them.

Academic evidence

The academic evidence is mixed and dated, with most studies carried out in the 1970s and 1980s when the broadcast environment was far less cluttered than it is today.

Most research confirmed that the programme context was important at the time and that advertising recall varied according to the environment in which it was shown. But conclusions were mixed.

A review of about 70 studies found that results usually depended on how the questions were asked: those supporting the Negative Effects Hypothesis, for example, tended to use laboratory-type approaches involving forced exposure in artificial environments amongst very small, non-projectable samples. Those endorsing the Positive Effects Hypothesis were backed up by real-world studies based on larger and more representative samples.

Research amongst 470 female heads of household in the USA by the authors of the review[24] found unaided recall to advertising to be 21% greater in high- versus low-involvement programmes, while aided recall scores were 59% higher.

Other work found that context was specific to individual programmes rather than broad genres – not all police dramas or sitcoms, for example, are the same. But the general conclusion was that high-attention programmes had a positive impact on the advertising within them – at least during the 1970s and 1980s.

Industry studies

Several media agencies,[25] have carried out work in this area. The consensus findings from this work were that:

- There is a difference between the power of individual programme environments to deliver impact that goes beyond a simple ratings count.
- The Positive Effects Hypothesis holds.
- A good surrogate measure for programme attention or involvement is the proportion of total minutes viewed.

Television stations,[26] have also looked at the subject of programme involvement and its relationship to commercial recall, concluding, similarly, that attentive programme viewers are more likely to remember commercials.

In the United States, syndicated services like TVQ and Nielsen IAG evaluate programmes according to their level of viewer appeal or engagement.[27] They, too, find a positive relationship between programme engagement and advertising recall.

The advertising environment

People watch television in all sorts of different situations. Regardless of the programme environment, these situations can have an effect on people's level of attentiveness to the screen. Whether they are watching at home, in a bar or at somebody else's home, for example, can affect their level of attentiveness. The fact that they may be watching alone or in company can also have an impact.

Advertising attentiveness can be affected by a range of other factors such as whether or not they are actually interested in the product category being advertised (e.g. if they are planning to buy a car or go to the movies), the time of day it is on, the day of the week or just the mood they are in.[28] Advertising recall – usually the measure being used interchangeably for 'effectiveness' – can also be affected by whether or not they have seen a commercial in the past.

But whatever the programme and viewing context, it remains true that most commercials appear between or amongst other commercials and that these commercials represent the main environment in which viewers see advertising. In recent years, in almost every country around the world, the amount of advertising that viewers are exposed to has grown considerably. The environment for watching advertising, in short, has become far more cluttered.

Complaints about too much advertising are not new. In an essay published in *The Idler* in 1759, Samuel Johnson wrote that:

> Advertisements are now so numerous that they are very negligently perused and it is therefore become necessary to gain attention by magnificence of promises, and by eloquence sometimes sublime and sometimes pathetic.

Television channels in many countries devote a considerable part of their broadcast output to commercial messages. This is how they earn a living. Few, however, can beat the United States for the sheer volume of commercial content.

TNS Media Intelligence reported that, in the third quarter of 2008, an *average* hour of prime time network programming in the USA contained 9 minutes of 'in-show brand appearances', as well as 13 minutes and 41 seconds of network commercial messages. Combined, this 22.41 minutes of marketing content represented 38% of a prime time hour.

Another company, Nielsen IAG, which tracks product placement appearances on screen, noted that in the fourth quarter of 2008, 745 brands appeared in prime time programmes on the broadcast networks – up by 73 from the previous year. On cable networks, 839 brands with in-programme placement appeared in prime time, a rise of 265 over the previous year.

This was prime time. The share of broadcast time devoted to commercial messaging of one sort or another is even higher in the late-night and daytime schedules.

The United States does not place any legal restrictions on the amount of commercial time television networks can run. In Europe, limits are imposed. The *EU Television Directive* of 1989 permits an average of 9 minutes per hour to be devoted to advertising (15% of broadcast time) and a maximum of 12 minutes (20%).

In Asia, some countries regulate advertising time and others don't – but the amount of commercial content generally lies somewhere in between the United States and Europe.

Faced with this clutter, viewers may choose to ignore advertising completely using their remote controls to switch channels or mute the sound. Or they may fast-forward through commercials if they have recorded programmes and played them back later. They can also leave the room or simply turn their attention elsewhere.

Do people skip advertising? Does it matter?

There are two ways in which the extent of ad skipping can be identified. First, we can examine behaviour: the extent to which people physically *avoid* advertising by switching channels, muting the set or fast-forwarding through commercials when playing back previously recorded programmes.

The second way is to look at evidence on viewer *recall* of advertising when audience measurement services report them as in the room or watching when advertising airs. This depends on their state of mind at the time a break plays and their general attitude towards commercials.

Remote control units were clumsy, awkward devices when they were initially adopted for television sets in 1950. The first one was attached to the set with a wire that was liable to trip viewers up, while early wireless units suffered from the drawback that channels could change randomly according to the amount of sunlight in a room.

They started dropping in price in the 1960s but really began to take off when infrared devices replaced ultrasonic units in the early 1980s. 29% of households in the United States had a remote control when Nielsen carried out its first survey in 1985.

Remote controls are almost universal in television households now. They enable people, should they so choose, to switch channels whenever commercials appear without leaving the comfort of their seat. Or they can simply press the mute button and carry on a conversation or do something else.

There has been no systematic research on the extent to which they do this. Audience measurement services don't report on usage of the mute button. And for technical reasons, rapid channel switching is usually not reported either, as a viewer needs to stay tuned to a channel for a certain amount of time before being registered as 'viewing' that channel.

When they are switching, but not remaining with any single channel for more than a few seconds, the peoplemeter assumes that they have not changed channels at all (see above). This may lead the meter to record viewing of commercials which did not in fact take place.

In North America, where the audience measurement services have historically focused on reporting average programme ratings, rather than audiences during the actual minutes that commercials air, a number of studies have been carried out into channel switching.

The studies showed a small net loss of audience between the programme and commercial minutes, which varied by age, sex and channel (people switched into breaks as well as switching out of them). But they did not address the issues of muting or rapid channel switching.

The extent of ad skipping, it can be concluded, is not yet effectively picked up by the mainstream peoplemeter technology.

VCRs

The next potential ad avoidance technology to arrive was the Video Cassette Recorder, introduced to the world's consumers in the mid-1970s.

By 1985, 14% of US households had installed a VCR, growing to 91% by 2004. Other countries saw similar growth rates and very high household penetration by the end of the twentieth century.

At the time VCRs were introduced, broadcast executives believed they marked the death of television. Viewers, it was feared, would record programmes and replay them without ever watching the commercials. As a result, advertisers would desert the medium, programme investment budgets would dry up and it would be the end of life as they knew it.

It didn't happen. Viewers found the recording functions complex and ended up using VCRs more for playing rented tapes than they did for recording on-air programmes and watching them later.

It was estimated that even at the height of VCR ownership in the United States, only around half of the programmes recorded were ever played back.[29] In the UK the figure was about a third.

This was not accounted for in the US viewing figures however, because all programmes that were recorded were assumed to have been viewed in the Nielsen ratings reports.

In the UK, this was not considered an acceptable assumption by the industry. TV audience measurement organisation BARB (the Broadcasters' Audience Research Board), therefore began incorporating a measure of VCR playback into the audience ratings in 1991.

In the end, though, VCR playback did not have a big impact on viewing levels. On average, it was found that just 2% of viewing overall was accounted for by VCR playback within seven days of the original broadcast – although for some types of programme – such as soaps and other dramas – the difference in viewing was sometimes as much as 15%. The figures also showed that two-fifths of playback viewing occurred on the day of transmission.

DVD Players/recorders and video games

The VCR has been on the decline for several years now, replaced with slicker DVD players and recorders. Like VCRs, DVD recorders can be used either to timeshift live television or to watch rented or purchased DVDs; the same methods developed for VCRs can be used to measure any recording and playing back of live broadcasts – although viewing of rented or purchased material is not usually included in viewing statistics.

In 2007 some 70% of all European households and 85% of US households were equipped with a DVD player/recorder.[30]

According to the Entertainment Software Alliance's *2008 Essential Facts About the Computer and Video Games Industry* in the United States, some 65% of American households play computer or video games. 39% of them have a dedicated games console.

22 million consoles had been sold in the UK by January 2009, enough for one to be in eight out of every ten households – though many own several. A similar picture exists in many other countries – notably in Japan.

Personal Video Recorders

In 1999, Personal Video Recorders or PVRs* were introduced in the United States. PVRs, like VCRs, enabled users to record live television and to play it back at a later date.

But they offer a number of significant advantages over VCRs. First, people can search for and record programmes up to several days ahead via a user-friendly electronic programme guide. An engineering degree is not required for setting up the recording operation.

---

* Also called Digital Video Recorders (DVRs) or Digital Television Recorders (DTRs).

Second, no tapes are involved. Instead, all programmes are recorded digitally onto a hard drive.

Third, PVRs empower viewers to 'pause' live television and to fast-forward or skip through advertisements when they are playing back what they have recorded. So by simply recording a programme and then starting to watch it, say, 15 minutes after its 'live' start, a viewer is technically able to watch the programme in almost real-time, skip the commercial breaks and finish watching as the programme ends its live transmission.

Not for the first time, it is feared that the end of commercial television as we know it has arrived. As soon as people experience a PVR, it has been said, they want one. And as soon as they have one, they don't know how they ever lived without it. And, of course, as soon as they can avoid irritating commercials with ease, they will.

US network ABC feared that, even if consumers initially chose to get PVRs for their ability to facilitate on-demand viewing, eventually they would get accustomed to the idea of zapping commercials as a by-product of the experience.[31] As sales chief Mike Shaw commented: '... we're just training a new generation of viewers to skip commercials because they can'.

But while there is no doubt that PVRs enable viewers to skip advertising, they clearly don't force them to do so.

Broadcasters clearly hope that people will continue to want to view mainly live material; watching television, they argue, is by and large a 'lean back' experience and will not suddenly become a 'lean forward' activity where viewers must work to see what they want.

Even when they do record programmes for later viewing, they may be quite happy sitting back and watching commercials most of the time. When they don't, they will have to watch the screen while they are fast-forwarding anyway, so will still be exposed to advertising messages at some level.

So what have we learned so far about this new technology?

Firstly, PVRs are not yet (in 2009) a global phenomenon. In the United States and the UK, they have certainly grown rapidly in popularity and are approaching the kind of critical mass where the behaviour of households which have them will have a significant impact on overall viewing statistics.

Nielsen in the United States reported that 31% of households there owned PVRs at the end of March 2009, up from less than 2% in 2003. In the UK, the comparative figure was around 30% in May 2009.

Statistics on household penetration in most countries are not published. But it does seem like the rest of the world has yet to reach these kinds of ownership levels, although they look set to catch up over the next few years.

IMS Research noted that PVR shipments in Europe in 2007 were running at about half the level in the USA,[32] but had almost doubled versus the previous year. Asia-Pacific remained a small, but fast-growing market.

The company forecasts that Europe and the USA will each share about one third of global PVR shipments by 2013.

It was expected when the devices were introduced that several things would happen. First, PVR users would watch more television. Not just because they were already heavier-than-normal viewers (which is why the PVR might have appealed to them), but because the choices and convenience offered by the technology would lead them to watch more than they used to. Lighter viewers would watch more for the same reason.

Second, people were expected to watch more attentively when they played back recorded programmes, because this viewing would be more of a planned event; they were sitting down to watch programmes they had specifically chosen to watch rather than just surfing or looking for the least worst thing showing that night.

Third, they would skip commercials whenever they could, in order to maximise viewing of what they had chosen to watch – because it was easy.

There are two ways to verify which – if any – of these has occurred. People can be asked in surveys about their behaviour or their viewing can be electronically tracked.

Viewer surveys

In early 2005 about 4% of UK households had a PVR. Ipsos's Digital Audience Research Tracker (DART) at the time reported that 90% of PVR users (97% of 16–34 year-olds) claimed to fast-forward through ads either 'always' or 'almost always', a figure that was higher than reported in a similar survey six months previously. This suggested that the behaviour would increase over time as people got used to the PVR's features.

Media agency Starcom polled 1,400 Sky Digital Homes in 2005, half of them with a PVR and half without, to see if ownership and usage had any impact on advertising awareness.

They had estimated from earlier surveys that viewers skipped through around three-quarters of ads in recorded programming and approximately 17% of ads in live programming (using the pause function). Combined with increased overall levels of viewing in PVR households it was calculated that they saw around 30% fewer ads than non-PVR households.

Across 58 TV campaigns and 18 sponsorships, it was found that overall advertising recall was 17% lower, although there was no significant drop-off in awareness of sponsorship messages (which tend to be used as signposts for the end of an ad break).[33]

US research commissioned by Lifetime television in early 2005 found that 99% of PVR users 'skipped advertising where possible', although 94% could still recognise individual brands in fast-forward mode.

A study by DoubleClick in 2008, also in the USA, reported that only 35% of PVR owners paid even occasional attention when watching ads on TV, and that more than half of them 'always' fast-forwarded through commercials.

In Canada, on the other hand, a 2008 study from the Television Bureau of Canada reported that 98.8% of television viewing was live and that three-quarters of those who did view in playback mode reported they were aware of the commercials they were fast-forwarding through or skipping.

As well, of those who use PVRs to fast-forward or skip ads, more than half say they will stop to watch commercials they find interesting or entertaining.

It is difficult to judge the extent to which these kinds of survey can truly reflect the on-going behaviour of PVR households. There is certainly an issue with how long ago the surveys were carried out – PVRs are becoming more and more 'normal' and less of an oddity. It is also important to distinguish between people who are recent purchasers and those who are experienced users, as behaviour is likely to be different.

And questions about what people 'sometimes' or 'always' do can be misleading – better for generating headlines than at capturing actual behaviour. A study that asks if somebody 'sometimes' fast-forwards or 'sometimes' watches ads does not establish the incidence of either.

Finally – with all the above in mind – it is important to keep a wary eye on who is funding the survey. Broadcasters are keen for advertisers to believe that it's business as usual, playing down any behaviour that might undermine the traditional commercial television model – viewers watch ads as the price of 'free' television.

Media agencies, conversely, are keen to show that the world is getting more and more complex, the old models are broken or damaged and that advertisers need their expertise to guide them through it.

Electronic tracking

Another approach is to record behaviour, rather than asking people to tell interviewers what they do. The viewing records of PVR owners can be directly monitored through the set-top boxes themselves or devices connected to them.

US PVR provider TiVo was the first to do this. In a major study, the company tracked 11,000 of its 'early adopter' households over several months during the 2002/03 programme season in the United States. They found that around two-thirds of prime time shows were watched in playback. The *average* commercial break was skipped in 54% of cases, and was particularly marked in the most highly involving programmes.

But as PVRs have reached beyond the early adopters towards a more mainstream audience, they do seem to have had a positive effect on the total amount of viewing a household records.

In the UK, the main PVR supplier, BSkyB, operates a panel of 20,000 of its subscribers. The panel shows that, when a new home signs up for the company's Sky+ PVR, they watch about 14% more commercial television than they watched previously.

About 87% of all the viewing on the set attached to the PVR remains to 'live' television while, of the remainder – which is time-shifted – a little over half (56%) of the ads are skipped. The net effect of this growth in total viewing and the fairly high incidence of ad skipping is, in fact, that slightly more ads are seen by new subscribers to PVRs than were seen before they had the device. This, of course, assumes that viewing to other sets in the household remains unchanged, which is by no means proven one way or the other.

Official UK audience measurement body BARB calculates that in PVR homes, time-shift represented around 17% of all viewing in May 2009 – which equates to about 5% of viewing across all households.

In the United States, TiVo's StopWatch service introduced in early 2007 also measures the second-by-second tuning behaviour of 20,000

PVR-equipped households. In January 2009 it reported that six of the seven network season premieres airing that month drew at least half of their audiences from time-shifted viewing, with some shows attributing as much as two-thirds of their audiences to non-live viewing.[34]

A substantial proportion of time-shifted viewers chose to watch these programmes more than 3 days after they aired, which places a question mark on whether including time-shifted audiences in overall programme audience estimates only if they are viewed within 3 days of transmission (the practice in the United States) is appropriate.

In fact, there is no longer a single way of estimating audiences to television programmes and commercials; Nielsen has, since 2007, offered its users several options. They may elect to look only at live viewing at the time of broadcast, at viewing which includes both live and time-shifted viewing after 3 days (known as C3) or at viewing which includes time-shifting after 7 days (C7). C3 is the dominant transaction currency for advertisers buying commercial airtime.

Finally, it is worth noting that the very act of fast-forwarding a commercial involves attending to what is on the screen to ensure that the programme is not cut into. This, it is argued, means that all commercials are seen to some extent (perhaps to a greater extent than in non-PVR households, where viewers could be out of the room or talking during a commercial break without affecting the ratings calculation). It also puts a premium on ad positions towards the end of a break.

Research sponsored by television stations in both the UK and US markets confirms that even ads that are fast-forwarded can be recalled, with viewers having to pay attention to what is on the screen in order to stop fast-forwarding before the programme resumes.[35]

Research with a small sample of PVR and non-PVR users in the United States in 2008 sought to uncover some of the reasons why this happened through applying biometric and eye-tracking techniques to the sample during viewing of a new programme with advertising inserted.[36]

It concluded that people who fast-forwarded ads tended to give far greater attention to the centre of the screen during fast-forwarding, enabling them to see what was being advertised and, especially when it was a commercial they had seen previously, to recognise the advertising and to recall the brand.

A large number of research studies have been carried out into the behaviour of viewers with Personal Video Recorders during the short life of the technology. The balance of the evidence to date is that it does seem to encourage people to watch more television, but that they do make use of the fast-forward button to skip advertising.

It is also true that PVR users are more active viewers in many ways. They are watching programmes they specially want to watch, presumably with minimum distraction. And they need to be attentive when they fast-forward in order to know when a commercial break ends.

The PVR has the potential to significantly upset the existing ad-supported business model the television has enjoyed for more than fifty years. Combined with the gradual introduction of television via broadband internet, enabling the streaming or downloading of television content with or without advertising, nothing short of a revolution is in prospect.

Catch-up TV

At the end of 2007, the BBC in the UK launched its iPlayer, a device that allowed viewers to 'catch-up' with any BBC programme they may have missed in the previous seven days by streaming it ('click to play') to their computers, some mobile phones or games consoles or by downloading it for up to 30 days. A year later, it was reported that around 180 million programmes had been watched over the player.

In March 2008, Hulu launched its video-streaming service in the United States. A year later, it was estimated that more than 24 million Americans used the service to watch video content on their computers from more than 130 'content partners' including broadcast networks NBC and Fox (ABC programmes are also now available on the site).

The Hulu library contains over 40,000 videos and, in February 2009, recorded 308 million streams from its users.[37] 80% of its streams carry advertising – which cannot be skipped.

Viewers can also pay to download their favourite shows or movies to watch at their convenience and without advertising from sources such as the iTunes store in the United States. It claimed in October 2008 to have sold more than 200 million TV episodes on its site.

The BBC's iPlayer and Hulu are just the largest of several internet-based services that allow viewers to source programming outside the normal broadcast schedule. Video content can also be watched via services like YouTube, which offers user-created videos.

All are competing for viewer attention in a rapidly changing and expanding world of video content. All are challenging 'traditional' audience measurement approaches. They are not viewed on television sets by and large, but on PCs or mobile devices. As a result they are measured in different ways (see Chapter 6).

Convergence

But there's more. For several years, companies have experimented with turning the television set from a 'dumb' receiving device, where viewers can watch live or pre-recorded programming to an 'intelligent' one, where they can use it to surf the web, order things and so on.

Interactive television services were introduced in the UK by the BBC in 1998. Viewers were invited to 'press the red button' on their screens if they wanted to find out more information about a programme or advertisement being aired.

An example of the technology in use occurred during the 2008 Beijing Olympic Games, where the Sport Multiscreen service offered red button users up to six different streams, plus news, results and statistics.

Other broadcasters in the UK and around the world have also experimented with similar technologies, though the availability of programmes and information to download from the internet has to some extent prevented these services from taking off in a big way.

Alternative ways of taking viewers' attention from the programmes and advertisements broadcasting live on their televisions are now being introduced by companies keen on bringing internet functionality direct to the television screen.

Most recently – in early 2009 – Samsung and other manufacturers began marketing television sets with pre-loaded applications which allow viewers to interact directly with the web without needing to switch out of the programmes they are watching. They can re-size the television picture while viewing and use different internet applications whenever they wish, connecting the set either by wire or wirelessly.

Although it is probable that they can already switch their attention from the set to their PCs whenever they wish, the ability to do so without the need for another screen may lead to more of this behaviour – especially during commercial breaks.

It is too early to judge the effect this will have on engagement with television commercials. The fact that it is on the same device will allow them to keep the pictures and sound on and will keep their eyes on the screen – a positive outcome for advertisers. But if the ease with which they can do so increases this kind of behaviour, then the impact is likely to be negative.

It is analogous to the transition from VCRs to PVRs: internet on the television is a service viewers can probably be persuaded they want, but they may be cautious given that it has historically been difficult to access. Once the difficulties are overcome, behaviour is likely to change.

The dizzying array of technologies reviewed here, from remote controls through VCRs, DVD players and PVRs to 'intelligent' sets which bring the internet to the living room television, all offer potential distractions from what broadcasters are airing to viewers. The many new choices available, from more channels to different viewing options, all lead in the same direction: fewer programmes reaching mass audiences as they are broadcast.

It is the job of audience measurement to capture these changes and record what people are doing. It also raises the question of how important these changes will be for the advertisers that fund the bulk of television activities across the world and, indirectly, the audience research that underpins the medium's appeal to them. What will happen, for example, when they can no longer reach mass audiences through a relatively small number of spots?

Do high-rated programmes deliver a better bang for the advertiser's buck?

Back in 1980, when the UK had just a single commercial channel, most of Europe's commercial television industries were tightly regulated and even US viewers could receive only ten channels on average, individual programmes could easily capture ratings in excess of 20 or even 30.

In the 1950s, historic American shows like *I Love Lucy* regularly topped the viewer rankings with more than half of television households tuning in. Since then, even the highest rated programmes achieve far lower audiences than they once did, as Table 5.3 shows.

Over this time, the number of channels available to people across the globe has grown exponentially. Most householders in the developed world

Table 5.3 Top rated US programmes, 1950–2008*

Programme season	Top programme	% of TV households tuned#
1950/51	Texaco Star Theater	62
1955/56	$64,000 Question	48
1960/61	Gunsmoke	37
1965/66	Bonanza	32
1970/71	Marcus Welby	30
1975/76	All in the Family	30
1980/81	Dallas	34
1985/86	The Cosby Show	34
1990/91	Cheers	21
1995/96	ER	22
2000/01	Survivor	17
2005/06	American Idol	18
2008	American Idol	16

* Includes only regularly scheduled programmes (e.g. not the Superbowl or other one-
off events)
To an average minute of the programme

Source: Nielsen

now own several colour television sets, almost all have remote control
devices for navigating between all the new channels and an increasing
number have VCRs, DVD players or Personal Video Recorders, which
can help them schedule their own viewing.

The result of all this has been a dramatic decline in the number of
high-rating programmes available for advertisers to buy into. This is true
worldwide, but particularly in the more advanced industrial nations.

In the UK, for example, almost two-thirds of programmes on the
country's largest commercial channel, ITV, generated less then 0.5 adult
ratings in 2005.

In the USA, an analysis of Nielsen Media Research data by OMD[38]
found that just 36 of the 3,435 programmes picked up by the audience
measurement service in March 2003 recorded more than 5 ratings.

By early 2009, only about 15 programmes on a weekly basis were
watched by more than 5% of the US population (these figures include
any PVR playback on the same day as the programme aired).

This is no doubt particularly low due to the sheer amount of choice available there – with more than 100 channels receivable by the average household. 30 or more programmes in the UK tend to be watched by more than 10% of the population though this, too, is far lower than it once was.

Many senior marketers today were schooled in an era of bigger ratings and more shared viewing experiences. Particularly in North America, there is a feeling amongst these professionals that it is important for their brands to have a presence in the dwindling number of higher rated programmes, because they are perceived to be somehow of greater 'quality'. This, in turn, leads to demand for slots in these shows exceeding supply, driving up the cost of advertising.

But is there any reason to believe that a higher rated programme is qualitatively – as well as quantitatively – superior to a lower rated one? In other words, is a 10 rating programme worth *more* than 10 times as much as a one rating programme to an advertiser?

There are several ways to look at the data on this. Do high-rating programmes, for example, help drive higher overall schedule reach for an advertiser? It stands to reason that they are, by definition, reaching more different people per commercial spot – a 10 rating slot will reach 10% of a given population, whereas there are likely to be some people who watch both of any 2 × 5 rating programmes – meaning that the total reach of the two lower rated programmes will be less than 10%.

But definitive data has yet to be produced that establishes a correlation between the schedule reach potential of higher versus lower average rated programme mixes. Turner Broadcasting in the USA were able to confirm in a detailed analysis carried out in 2002 that a wide range of different schedules with similar total ratings levels and daypart mixes but different average spot rating levels showed no difference in schedule reach performance.

Another possible factor differentiating high- and low-rated programmes is the level of attention paid by viewers. One could hypothesise that high-rated programmes are the ones people tend to talk about with each other at work and school and so are likely to be more closely attended to.

Nielsen Media Research examined the amount of channel switching occurring in different programmes as a surrogate for attentiveness back in 1990. The greater the level of switching, it was assumed, the lower the level of attentiveness. The company did find a relationship between rating size and the number of switching occasions: the higher the rating, the less the amount of switching.[39] However, as noted above, the peoplemeter is an imprecise measurement yardstick, which fails to pick up rapid channel switching. And in 1990, channel choice was far more limited, PVRs nearly a decade away and the internet still tiny.

Another way of tackling the same question is through surveys. Attentiveness studies have, over the years, shown clearly that attention levels do vary between shows, although generally these studies only ask about the most popular programmes, drawing no firm conclusions about the high/low debate.

Another confirmation of the lack of any correlation between audience size and audience attentiveness comes from US company, Nielsen IAG Research. For several years, they have polled several thousands of viewers on-line daily, inviting them to take part in mini-quizzes about programmes and commercials they claimed to have seen on the previous evening.

Each viewer of a 30-minute programme is asked eight questions about what they remember of the episode. If, on average, viewers of that show answer four out of eight questions correctly, the episode will earn a Programme Engagement Score of 50%. Every episode is measured and these scores are then combined to create Programme Engagement Scores for every programme, programme type and major network.

Analysis of the company's substantial database found no relationship between Programme Engagement Scores and audience size – although it did find a strong correlation between programme engagement and advertising recall.[40]

The answer to the question of whether high ratings deliver a better bang for the advertiser's buck is therefore 'not necessarily'. Factors other than audience size are likely to be far more important in determining whether viewers recall advertising.

The daypart in which an ad appears, the proportion of a programme watched, how much it is enjoyed or attended to and the creative strength of the commercial itself are more important.

But other considerations often come into play in constructing schedules for advertisers. In many product markets it is important for a marketer to achieve 'visibility' amongst suppliers and distributors, a difficult concept to define using hard data. The default measurement for 'talkability' is ratings.

In the UK, television marketing organisation Thinkbox argues this case strongly: 'What's happening on Coronation Street or in the Big Brother House fuels conversation at home, at work, at school. TV can gel even the most diverse group. And when a TV ad ignites people's imagination, it becomes as much a part of the current culture as any programme.'[41]

On a final note, it is worth pointing out that the issue of statistical accuracy is becoming more important as the average audiences to programmes continue to decline. There are currently about 9,500 adults on the UK BARB TV audience measurement panel. As noted above, the vast majority of programmes recorded by BARB generate ratings of less than 0.5. A 0.5 rating equates to about 47 people. As buyers look beyond the first to the second decimal point for evaluating airtime purchases, we face an era of lower and lower sample sizes on which to base multi-million dollar investment decisions.

Other television research

Assuming an advertising break is not skipped, the key media influences on recall of a commercial within it will include:

- its position within the break;
- the number of other commercials around it;
- the length of the break;
- the position of the break within a programme;
- whether the break appears within or between programmes.

A study by billetts in the UK[42] addressed many of the key questions concerning the importance of break position and other factors to advertising recall.

A larger scale project carried out by the Cable Advertising Bureau in the USA confirmed the billetts findings that the highest recall occurred for commercials:

- in early positions within the break;
- in shorter breaks;
- with fewer competing commercials.

There has been a clear trend over the past 40 years to running shorter-length television commercials.

In 1965, 77% of all US network television commercials lasted 60 seconds, a share which dropped to 27% five years later and has since fallen to 8% (2008).

30-second ads made up 23% of the total in 1965 and 72% in 1970, but had fallen back to 56% by 2008. 15-second units, introduced in the late 1980s, made up a third of all messages by this date.

In the UK, similar trends towards downsizing spot lengths have been apparent. 30-second ads already made up two-thirds of the total by 1972, while those lasting 15 seconds represented a further 20%. By 2005, 30-second spots constituted 45% of the UK total, 15-second ads had virtually disappeared and 10- and 20-second spot lengths each made up around one fifth of the total.

It is one of the truisms in media planning that bigger is (usually) better. In print, for example, double-page spreads tend to be recalled better than full-page advertisements, while larger poster sizes do better than smaller ones. In the same way, almost all of the research into people's recall of television advertising has found longer length commercials scoring more highly than shorter ones.

But the relationship is not linear. Recall studies have shown that cutting the length of an advertising message in half may halve the cost of a commercial, but will generally result in only a slight loss in the ability of that commercial to register in the consumer's memory. Belief in this general formula held throughout the 1970s, 1980s and 1990s, as average spot lengths declined.

But the substantial increase in commercial clutter and general noise has arguably given reason for marketers to pause in their quest for increased efficiency through shorter and shorter messages. Greater channel choice, viewing fragmentation, channel switching and busier lifestyles have all conspired to reduce the amount of fully attentive viewing going on. It is possible that shorter length commercials could more easily be missed in this environment.

A BBC research study in the UK, for example, found people's attention to the television set generally had declined quite sharply between 1974 and 2002;[43] in 1974 some three-quarters of viewing was considered to be a 'primary activity'. 28 years later less than half of all viewing was placed into this category by viewers.

UK broadcasters – though not yet their US counterparts – have also got wise to the trend by raising the relative price of shorter length

Table 5.4 Index of recall by commercial break position (5-commercial pods only)

Position in break	1st	2nd	3rd	4th	5th
Index	125	116	84	67	104

NB: All commercials within 5-commercial pods = 100

Source: Nielsen/Cable Television Advertising Bureau, 2000

commercials – a 10-second spot, for example, costs half as much as a 30-second spot, not one third as much.

Most studies into the relative effectiveness of different time lengths have been based on unaided (spontaneous) or aided recall, where viewers are contacted shortly after a commercial has run and asked whether they can remember details such as the brand name or key copy points.

In the 1960s and 1970s many of these studies were run in the United States. The general finding from the aided recall research was that a 30-second ad generated 75–80% of the recall levels achieved by a 60-second ad. The loss was greater when brand names were asked about spontaneously. When it came to comparing the recall levels of 30-second versus 15-second ads, further drops of similar magnitude were recorded.[44]

ZenithOptimedia's UK *Persistence* Study in 1999 found a 15% drop in awareness between 30- and 10-second spots running in prime time, far less steep than the 50% drop recorded in the company's US study. The decline between 30s and 15s in the latter research had been just 20%, suggesting that there is a point beyond which the message was simply not getting through in the relatively more cluttered US market.

Billetts' *Share of Break* (1992) and *Commercial Break Ecology* (1998) studies in the UK both confirmed the US finding that recall levels fell as the spot length was reduced. But there was no sign that 10-second ads were being completely lost, as had seemed to be happening in the USA.

New research has not been carried out for some years into whether the assumption still holds as strongly as it did and may need to be repeated. Can a 10- or 15-second commercial still tell its story effectively in the age of the Personal Video Recorder and internet television, when so many other things are competing for viewers' attention?

Measuring return on investment

Companies invest money in advertising in the expectation that it will help them to sell more of their product, sell the same amount at a higher price, or some combination of the two. One way or the other, they hope to make more in additional revenue than they spend on the advertising.

But a study by Deutsch Bank[45] in 2004 reported that several well-known consumer packaged goods (CPG) companies in the United States advertising their brands on television were not making a positive cash return on their investments.

The bank examined 23 household, personal-care, food and beverage brands over three years, looking at both the short-term (six months) and longer-term (12 months) effects of television advertising.

This long-term analysis is important, as many advertising effects can last far longer than the immediate period following a campaign. If, for example, somebody is persuaded to change the brand of soap or razor blade they buy after seeing some advertising, it is a brand they may then continue with. This means that the advertising they saw originally has effects that persist long into the future.

According to the Deutsch Bank analysis, almost all the brands showed a positive lift in sales volumes over the six months following the advertising. But less than one fifth (18%) succeeded in generating a positive *cash* return on their investment in the short term – defined as the gross profit they earned on every sale multiplied by the number of extra sales generated by the advertising and then compared with the cost of the advertising. Worse, less than half (45%) of the brands saw their TV investment pay off, even when incremental revenues were analysed over a full year.

There were plenty of caveats to this analysis. Non-television advertising was not taken account of, neither was the analysis extended beyond a year. The relative strength of the different creative messages employed were not evaluated. And, vitally, the advertising costs used were not actual costs, but a set of industry-estimated costs which are generally accepted as being much higher than the real costs paid. Non-CPG product categories were not examined at all. And, crucially, the negative impact of *not* advertising while competitive brands continued to do so was not considered.

But whatever the shortcomings of the report, the analysis touched a raw nerve amongst advertisers and pointed to the ways in which many companies were starting to measure the effectiveness of all their marketing investments. Surrogate measures, such as the number of people seeing their commercials, are just part of the picture in the twenty-first century.

The future of television audience measurement

It is clear from this chapter that television is a very different medium to the one advertisers flocked to in the 1950s. Viewers have much better television sets than they have ever had – and many have several.

Their choice of channels can now number several hundred in cable and satellite homes. Alternative uses for the television set including the watching of bought or rented DVDs, the playing of computer games, the pausing, recording and playing back of live television and, soon, access to the internet. It is changing its role from that of a 'dumb' box to one of an interactive entertainment centre.

That said, today – in 2009 – the household television set remains by far the primary means of accessing video content. The question is – will this change and, if so, how quickly.

Peoplemeter samples and technology are struggling to keep up, yet remain the principal 'currency' of advertising sales and marketing throughout the world. Passive measurement through portable peoplemeters or other devices has yet to attain credibility, while Return Path Data or RPD, is still at an early stage. Viewing of video on the internet or via mobile devices is measured using different methods.

RPD is likely to be the best answer to measuring the millions of individual behaviours that now characterise the television landscape, but only if enough people agree to have their viewing monitored like this (assuming they are asked) and providing that the various technical barriers are overcome.

Even then, measuring what is happening on the set will not be enough for advertisers. They also need to know who, if anybody, is attending to the sets when they are on. This behaviour may be captured by passive monitoring devices of one sort or another. There may also be a place for sampling modest numbers of viewers and modelling their behaviour onto the larger group of homes whose set-tuning behaviour is being captured automatically. At this point in time, we cannot yet claim to know the answer.

6 Measuring internet audiences

Nobody really knows how many people go to your web site.

Eric T. Peterson[1]

Introduction

The internet is a system which links networks of computers via a common set of standards and protocols allowing them to label, recognise and move data amongst themselves.

Various services use the internet, one of which is the world wide web, named and invented by Tim Berners-Lee and launched in 1991. His contribution was to design a global 'hypertext' system enabling people to access and share content.

A reported 1.6 billion people – almost a quarter of the world's population – were connected to the internet and able to access content on the web by March 2009. This was up from just 361 million in 2000.[2] In the most developed parts of the globe, penetration is far higher – 74% in North America and 49% in Europe for example. The greatest number of users are in Asia, with 300 million in China alone and a further 94 million in Japan.

Broadband internet, which refers to higher speed connections able to carry greater amounts of data, has also grown rapidly in recent years. Around 429 million broadband connections were reported at the end of March 2009, just under half of them in North America and Western Europe.[3]

It has been estimated that the sum total of all the content created, captured or replicated in digital form worldwide totalled about 281 exabytes in 2007[4] – one exabyte is the equivalent of 50,000 years of DVD-quality video. Indications are that the volume of digital content is growing very rapidly, with IDC forecasting it will increase more than six-fold in the four years from 2007 to 2011.

Not all of this content is necessarily stored on the world wide web. But plenty of it is. It consisted of more than 33 billion pages of content in May 2009,[5] with traffic growing by an estimated 50–60% a year.[6]

A growing role

The internet plays a major role in people's lives. At home, users spend an average of 78 minutes on-line every day in the United States, 70 minutes in the UK, 76 minutes in Germany and 81 minutes in France.[7]

It is used for three main purposes:

- For communication. People stay in touch with each other using email, chat and social networking sites such as Facebook and Twitter.
- For content. This ranges from news, sports, video and audio material through to business or other information, often accessed through search sites like Google, Yahoo and MSN.
- For commerce. Internet users can buy and sell goods and services on-line. They can also research products using Search, price comparison and review sites.

Advertising can – and has – carved out a role for itself within all three of these spheres. But the internet is different from other mainstream media. Where television takes the form of video, radio comes to us as audio and print as text – the internet is all these. It is an *environment* in which content can be accessed and shared which may come in audio, visual or textual forms.

And because the web contains content created by newspapers, magazines, film studios, television and radio stations, measurement of the audiences to any of this content accessed through the internet is becoming an important adjunct to or extension of traditional audience measurement services.

Television audience measurement services, for example, need to find ways of incorporating viewing via the internet, where people can stream or download programmes and advertising. The radio and print media, too, must find ways of quantifying the audiences they now attract through this new distribution channel.

As a medium, the internet has been able to exploit the equity built up over the years by many traditional media brands. When people go to the sites of newspapers like the *New York Times*, the UK's *Guardian* or France's *Le Figaro*, they know what they will get thanks to many years of building these brands off-line.

Evidence in recent years is that, while audiences to media content through some of the traditional distribution channels has been stagnating or even falling, the number of people accessing it through the internet has been increasing rapidly.

To take just two examples from the United States:

- In March 2007, 71% of internet users viewed around 7 billion videos for an average of just under 5 minutes daily according to comScore Video Metrix. Two years later, 78% of internet users viewed on-line video for an average of 11 minutes daily, watching between them some 14.5 billion videos. Compared with the total amount of television viewing, the internet's share is tiny – about 3% of all video consumption. But it more than doubled in volume over the two years to March 2009 and shows no sign of slowing.
- 73 million people – 44% of internet users – visited newspaper websites monthly in the first quarter of 2009 according to Nielsen Online. This was 10.5% higher than the same period in 2008. In contrast, the Audit Bureau of Circulations (ABC) reported that hard-copy newspaper circulations in the six months to March 2009 were down 7% year on year.

But despite this, not all of the traditional media have suffered equally. Reported television viewing levels in the United States and the UK, for example, have continued to grow over the past ten years.

Magazine readership levels in the United States, according to MRI, also showed a rise between 2004 and 2008, despite all the new opportunities offered by the internet[8] although circulations have fallen back slightly over the past ten years.

The internet is not merely a source of information. It can also be used as a mail service, a telephone, a social networking facility, a dating service, a photograph storage device, a retail channel and an advertising delivery mechanism. Measurement of all these activities is useful to many companies.

A brief history of the internet

The world's first operational 'packet-switching' network – the predecessor of the internet – was the ARPANET (Advanced Research Projects Agency Network) developed within the United States Department of Defense.

The ARPA had been set up in 1958 to support scientific research. Computer scientists supported by the agency worked from locations far from each other, each holding their own sets of data on computers that themselves were a relatively rare resource at the time. ARPA wanted them to communicate and share information more efficiently and encouraged efforts to help them do so.

The packet-switching method allowed data to be transmitted easily and securely by multiple parties using a shared communications link. It was similar to the way the postal system enabled people to mail letters to each other. Letters would start and end at millions of different locations, but they all used the same transport infrastructure and the same protocol for identifying each location – an address and zip code.

At the time, telephones used a finite number of dedicated circuits, each of which was used exclusively for an individual phone call and was therefore unavailable to other users for the duration of each phone call. This clearly limited its use for sharing large amounts of data on a regular basis.

Two computers, one at the University of California at Los Angeles (UCLA) and the other at the Stanford Research Institute near San Francisco were linked together using the new system, with the first message exchanged on-line on 29 October 1969.

The message was 'lo'. In fact, UCLA student Charley Kline was trying to communicate the word 'login', but the computer crashed before the 'g' transmitted. It was back up and running successfully shortly afterwards.

Over the next 20 years or so, computers became more accessible to people outside academia and communications protocols were developed and implemented. The first network email was sent out using ARPANET in 1971 – between two computers sitting next to each other. Two years later 75% of the network's traffic was email – the first 'killer app'.

In December 1974, three men at Stanford University made the first recorded use of the term 'internet' in a formal specification for a Transmission Control Protocol (TCP) that would standardise the way in which different computers communicated.

By 1992, most of the key technical barriers preventing computers talking to each other around the world had been successfully overcome; the next landmark occurred when Tim Berners-Lee published a paper that year proposing a 'world wide web' and coining the phrase 'surfing the internet'.

Key historical events in the life of the world wide web include:

- 1994: the first internet search engine, Yahoo, was launched;
- 1995: JavaScript was implemented in Version 2 of the Netscape browser, adding new functionality to web pages;
- 1995: eBay, which was to become the largest on-line person-to-person trading community, was set up;
- 1996: Microsoft introduced its free on-line browser, Internet Explorer;
- 1997: Jorn Barger coined the term 'weblog' (shortened to 'blog' two years later);
- 1998: Google launched its search engine;
- 2005: YouTube went live.

Advertising on the internet

As noted earlier, advertising has the potential to push itself into many corners of the internet experience, reaching people as they communicate with each other, as they search for information and as they execute commercial transactions.

The internet has been the fastest growing major advertising channel worldwide every year since 2002. Advertisers spent an estimated $50 billion in the medium in 2008.[9] In Denmark, the medium overtook television and newspapers in 2008 to become the largest single advertising medium.

Three major formats are offered: Search, Classified and Display advertising, as well as others such as email and 'lead generation' (e.g. when companies pay sites directly for qualified purchase enquiries) – see Table 6.1.

Table 6.1 Share of internet advertising expenditure by format, 2008

	USA	UK
Search	45%	59%
Display*	33%	19%
Classified	14%	21%
Lead generation	7%	–
Email	2%	< 1%
Total spend	$23.4 billion	$6.2 billion

*E.g. banner ads, rich media, digital video and sponsorship

Sources: IAB Internet Advertising Revenue Report (USA)/IAB Online Adspend Study 2008 (UK)

Search

In 2008 Search was easily the leading advertising format worldwide, representing 45%[10] of US on-line spending and 43% of European spending;[11] in the UK, Search accounted for a massive 59%[12] of the total.

It has become the dominant format very quickly. Back in 2001, according to Internet Advertising Bureau estimates, 'keyword search' accounted for just 4% of US internet advertising expenditure.

Companies like Google and Yahoo sell the rights for certain keywords or phrases to companies who want their ads to be featured and their sites to be prominent when users input the keywords into their search site.

So, for example, if somebody types the words 'luxury car' into Google, a list of car-related sites will come onto the screen alongside banner links in a column on the right-hand side of the screen.

The order and prominence with which they appear will be linked both to how much advertisers have bid for the keyword and the expected 'click-thru' rate for the ad. Because marketers only pay Google when users actually click on the text link, Google has a vested interest in featuring the most compelling ads high on its search results screen.

Display

Display advertising historically referred to static or hyper-linked 'banners' of all shapes and sizes that appeared on websites or popped up in front of surfers as they moved around the web. In 2001, 'banners and sponsorships' together accounted for 62% of spending in the United States.

Display now also refers to a number of other formats including so-called 'rich media', which incorporate sound, animation or interactivity. Running video commercials, for example, is an increasingly popular way to reach internet users.

Unlike on television, where arguably viewers could switch channels or, if they are playing commercials back on a Personal Video Recorder, could fast-forward through the ads, internet technology enables content owners to force them to watch – or at least to play – a short video advertisement before seeing the video content they have requested.

This is known as 'pre-roll'. (If the commercials are shown in the middle of the requested video or afterwards, it is referred to as 'mid-roll' or 'post-roll' respectively.)

Some sites offering video content give viewers a choice of whether to watch pre-roll commercials or normal advertising in return for free content. Others do not.

Email

Email continues to be a popular marketing communications channel for some companies due to its low cost-per-contact and ability to provide direct, measurable results.

Permission-based, or 'opt-in' email marketing, is seen as an important element in developing the approach. The choice of opting in or out of receiving marketing emails often occurs when, for example, an internet user signs up to an email newsletter or buys a product on-line.

People who sign up to receive a particular newsletter or bulletin (or, in the case of buying a product, either tick a box agreeing to receive marketing communications or fail to un-tick a pre-ticked box) are said to have opted in to receive it.

A 'double opt-in' occurs when they make the same request and later confirm it in response to a separate communication. Opting out, on the other hand, represents the specific action of a user wanting to be removed from an on-line communication of any sort – including receiving marketing messages of various kinds.

The extent to which either people or their computer firewalls prevent companies from contacting them electronically for marketing purposes will clearly have an impact on the effectiveness of email as a marketing method.

As in-boxes become more and more crowded with marketing messages and other unwanted materials, consumer attitudes and behaviour towards email marketing are likely to harden.

Audience measurement

In the mid–late 1990s, as the internet medium was beginning to emerge, it was able to tap into a strong desire amongst advertisers and their media agencies for a measurement approach that allowed them to link advertising investment directly to returns in the marketplace.

Traditional media, as we have seen, provided them with estimates of whether people had had an 'opportunity' to see their advertising – with no further information on whether this linked to subsequent buying behaviour.

The internet promised much more. It was awash with data on which people had seen which web pages, how long they spent on a site, whether they clicked on a banner ad – and whether they went on to order a product on-line.

As the internet business grew, so too did the measurement industry. Marketers were offered the opportunity to target consumers according to their behaviour and interests (as indicated by which sites they visited).

Customer 'journeys' towards purchasing a product or service could be traced through Search, product review and price comparison sites, noting whether or not they had been exposed to banner advertising along the way. And, of course, all this could be linked directly with a consumer action such as requesting a brochure, booking a test drive or even buying a product on-line.

The internet, its enthusiasts argued, offered a number of unique advantages over traditional advertising media:

- Every action taken by an internet surfer is tracked at some level, making it amongst the most measurable of media. All computers need an Internet Protocol or IP address in order for them to send and receive data, just as any individual needs a postal address to send and receive mail. Insofar as the data being sent to and from these addresses can be tracked, counted and identified with a person or prospect, measurement can take place.

- The internet's advantages are not only technical. People often use it specifically to research goods and services before they buy. When they browse price comparison or product review sites, or look up products or product categories via search engines, they are generally assumed to be 'in the market' to buy at some point – an important consideration for marketers. Being able to track them as they move from site to site gives marketers useful clues as to which sites are pivotal for pushing consumers to their own sites and brands.

- As well as using the internet to research and browse products, consumers are increasingly using it to make purchases directly. A survey by Nielsen Online in late 2007, for example, polled internet users in 48 countries around the world.[13] The study found that 86% of respondents had made purchases on-line at some point (more than twice as many as reported in a survey two years earlier). Key products purchased on-line included books (41%), videos, DVDs or games (24%), airline tickets or reservations (24%) and electronic equipment (23%).

It's not quite as simple ...

In fact, measuring internet audiences is not as straightforward as it seems at first glance. First of all, measuring the behaviour of machines is not the same thing as measuring the behaviour of people.

The technologies used (including computer IP addresses and internet 'cookies'), as well as the ways in which consumer behaviour is linked to their exposure to web advertising, are subject to a range of errors and interpretations as wide as any that exist in more traditional media measurement.

Also important is the continuing popularity of buying goods and services off-line. Much of the time, internet users research products on-line but still choose to purchase in traditional retail outlets. This makes the connection between what they see on the web and their purchase decision more difficult to establish.

The internet has spawned multiple approaches to measuring audiences to advertising and other content in its short history. These include surveys of behaviour, detailed tracking of page visits and time spent on sites and panels of users which enable advertisers to generate measures familiar to them in other media such as audience ratings, reach and frequency.

Surveys of behaviour

Surveys of consumers can be used to paint a picture of internet behaviour – asking people, for example, how often they use the internet in an average day or week, how long they spend on-line and which sites they visit. This can be particularly useful if internet usage is asked about alongside questions on other media (see Chapter 8).

On the other hand, as with any survey, it is important to be aware of the limitations of asking people about behaviour they may not necessarily want to be fully transparent about or which they may not be able to recall accurately. It is also difficult to capture the level of detail required by media planners and buyers on every site or page visited over a period of time.

It has been claimed, for example, that people under-report the total amount of television they actually view (watching too much television being considered as a 'bad' thing). In a similar vein, many survey respondents over-claim the share of their viewing going to programmes like news, current affairs and documentaries and under-represent the number of soap operas or other lowbrow shows they watch.

One way of verifying the claims people make in surveys is to observe them in their everyday lives – known as ethnography by market researchers. A large-scale ethnography study in the United States in 2008 found that, on average, people only watched about 2 minutes a day of video on their PCs.[14]

This, the authors suggested, showed that panels and surveys tended to exaggerate the amount of time people spend watching video on their PCs or mobile phones (which is considered to be more 'cool') and to under-report the amount of time they spent watching television.

Panel companies like comScore and Nielsen do, indeed, report far higher levels of on-line video viewing than the ethnography study suggested: putting it at around 7–10 minutes of viewing a day amongst the 50% of the population who use PCs to watch video.

In all kinds of market research, attempts are made to reduce bias as far as possible – ensuring that the people who take part in it are not predisposed in favour of or against certain behaviours.

It may be argued that the kinds of people who agree to have their actions watched for long periods by strangers with electronic 'clipboards', people prepared to have their PCs metered for long periods of time or even those taking part in on-line surveys, may not be entirely typical of the general population.

But whether or not survey estimates of on-line video viewing are precise, all show a firm and rapid upward trend. As on-line video usage grows, the estimates produced by different survey techniques may begin to converge.

Surveys can also help in probing why consumers act as they do. They assist in understanding how the internet is used in the researching and buying of certain products and services and whether it drives intent to purchase, brand or message awareness and so on – all of which are useful in complementing the main measurement metrics.

The principal continuous methods of measuring the internet audiences are known as 'site-centric', 'user-centric' and 'network-centric' approaches. More recently, 'hybrid' approaches which combine elements of the site-centric and user-centric methods, have been introduced.

Site-centric measurement

As noted earlier, internet traffic can be tracked to and from any IP address. This is done through 'cookies' – small text files placed and stored on a user's computer by a website server. Every visit to a web page is logged by the server hosting the page. Through installing these cookies, an IP address can be identified and recognised by the server every time it returns to a website previously visited.

This speeds up browsing, as many of the web files will have been stored on the user computer's 'cache' (i.e. its record of visited sites).

All cookies have an owner which tells you who the cookie belongs to. The owner is identified in the cookie file name. It is possible for these owners to be either 'first party' or 'third party' cookies, depending on whether they belong to the website itself or to another web operator.

When an internet surfer visits a particular site, a first-party cookie – usually with the name of the site in question – will be installed on the surfer's browser. But if the web page being viewed on the site also features content from a third-party domain such as that of an advertiser (whether or not the advertisement is clicked on) this will also install a cookie.

Because advertisements are served over multiple sites by the same third-party companies, these companies can then identify and track users as they move from site to site.

Making the picture even more complicated, within third-party cookies there is usually a random ID number placed within the cookie filename, which can allow the company to build up an anonymous profile of the sites visited by a particular user's computer.

This knowledge, in turn, enables a marketer to target messages to users according to the particular sites they visit. If, for example, they often visit movie-related sites, it may be concluded that they are interested in movies and so will be more receptive to movie advertising.

Three core metrics are used by websites to measure their audiences:

- *Unique visitors*: the number of individuals* who visit a site at least once in a given period;
- *Site visits*: the number of visits logged to a given website (usually consisting of multiple pages); and
- *Page views*: the number of times a page is viewed.

All these metrics have been defined and described by the Web Analytics Association and the Internet Advertising Bureau in the United States in an attempt to get everybody using the same measures.[15]

Individual websites offer all these data to advertisers and, in some countries, the information can be independently audited, providing media buyers and advertisers with a third-party validation of traffic to their sites.

This validation can be important for several reasons. Counting web page visits is not as straightforward as it sounds – it is not just people who click onto websites – page traffic can be enhanced by website development activity, by automated search engines, indexers, robots and spiders.

There is also the possibility of 'click fraud', where a person, automated script or computer program impersonates a legitimate user of a web browser clicking on an advertisement.

---

* Technically, the number of individual computer browsers, which may or may not be the same thing – see below.

This is one reason why the number of visitors and page impressions registered by web servers is generally much higher than the audiences reported by panels of users (see below), which focus on individuals rather than sites.[16]

Other reasons may include the existence of international traffic to a website (i.e. unrepresented by a national panel) and issues with cookie measurement (see below).

Web analytics

Analysis of site-centric data is known as web analytics. This describes ways in which visitors to a given website or set of websites behave – for example isolating the particular 'landing pages' they click on and gauging how effectively people are led to make purchases or provide information such as their email addresses. The performance of a given page or website can be compared with a database of other pages and sites and used to help the site owner make improvements.

Web analytics are used by marketers to identify the campaigns and strategies that are working best and also to help in targeting people according to their surfing behaviour.

They are also useful to website developers, who can observe how people navigate within and between sites, how long they spend on different pages and at different tasks and what seems to drive them towards and away from particular pages or websites.

Several different ways can be used to collect site audience data. For example 'logfiles' record all transactions on a website. Analysis of these files can be used to generate the metrics described earlier such as the number of page views and visits to a site, using cookies to try to exclude non-human activity.

A drawback of looking only at logfiles is that when pages are cached on a user's computer, the website may not register subsequent visits and will therefore under-count the audience. It is possible, however, to configure the web analytics system to make sure that this does not happen – effectively by telling the user's web browser to check the central server every time they request a page to see if it has been modified.

The alternative approach is to use page tagging or a 'web bug'. This is a small invisible image planted on the page which, again, causes the user's computer to re-contact the server every time they request a web page to retrieve certain information. This ensures they are registered as having looked at it.

Some people may choose to disable JavaScript, which is at the heart of the page-tagging approach, although this is thought to cover a small minority of users.

Attribution

Marketers, as well as website owners, use web analytics to help them identify how well campaigns are performing and which elements are working most effectively. As with so much about internet measurement, however, it is by no means simple for them to compute the returns on investment of their campaigns.

In theory, any on-line purchase or other consumer action can be credited to the on-line marketing exposures that preceded it. In practice, many marketers simply attribute the conversion to the so-called 'last click' – i.e. the exposure received by a consumer prior to the purchase.

Yet that same consumer may have been exposed to several other on-line marketing messages through a combination of Search, banner, email and other vehicles in the run-up to purchase.

Depending on the product type and how long campaigns have run, it may be useful to look back several weeks or months to gauge the extent to which these various influences have impacted the final purchase event.

Such a full-blown 'attribution' exercise is, in fact, rarely carried out by marketers, despite a range of tools being available for the purpose. The data available to execute such an analysis are not always complete or entirely accurate; however, it is an activity that several analysts believe will become increasingly common in on-line campaign analysis.[17]

Problems with cookies

Neither a computer's IP address nor cookies can identify an individual person, although it is commonly assumed that they do. A cookie is, in fact, associated with a combination of a user account, a computer and an internet browser.

At work, for example, the computers people use are likely to be associated with a company IP address, rather than with one specific to the individual. In households with multiple computers using the same cable modem, all the machines will share an IP address.

Several people may share a single user account, computer or browser. And one individual may use several computers or internet browsers. Somebody, for example, with separate home and work computers as well as mobile internet access, will generate three separate cookies when, of course, it is one and the same person.

Only in cases where a single computer is operated by a single individual at home using the same internet browser is it reasonable to assume, in most cases, that this person can be associated with a machine's IP address.

Another challenge for web analytics is cookie deletion. When a user deletes a cookie, he will appear as a new user on a site which he may already have visited, inflating the 'unique' audience numbers.

Visitor inflation is likely to be worse for sites that people go to on a daily basis (e.g. a news site) than it is for less frequented ones. Theoretically, if somebody deletes their cookies every day, they could be counted up to 30 times in a monthly unique visitor count.

On the other hand, cookie deletion underestimates the *frequency* of visits. Site owners might be interested in how often people return to them. But in the example above, daily visitors who delete their cookies 30 times a month will be adding plenty to the tally of 'unique' visitors and nothing to average visit frequency – which may have value to many site owners and advertisers.

The cookies being deleted or blocked tend to be third-party cookies, as opposed to less problematic first-party cookies which, if blocked, will make it very difficult to surf the internet. First-party cookies are necessary in order for a user to be recognised as an individual and are not targeted by anti-spyware software or privacy settings.

The extent of the cookie deletion effect will depend both on the periods used to analyse site visitors (longer periods will be subject to more frequent deletion and therefore greater error) and on how regularly people actually delete them.

Reports vary on how serious the incidence is. Research by both Jupiter and Nielsen in late 2004 and early 2005 suggested that, at that time, around 40% of users surveyed deleted cookies on a monthly basis.[18] A more recent study by comScore put the figure at a round a third.[19]

Cookies are the main way used by the industry to identify unique visitors – but not the only way. Some sites use registration data from purchases or user IDs from logins. This is more accurate, but covers only a minority of sites.

As can be seen, the principle of site-centric measurement is straightforward; in practice, it can be very complex to measure accurately.

User-centric measurement

The second main approach to measuring internet audiences is more in line with the those employed by other media. Panels of users are built that represent the internet population (at home and/or at work).

The people on the panels are tracked continuously to see which sites they visit, how long they stay and whether or not they make any purchases. Consumer 'journeys' can also be traced, looking at which sites they visit on the way to a purchase.

The goals of user-centric measurement are to measure:

- user activity – including the sites visited and the order in which they visit them;
- user behaviour – encompassing the amount of time spent on each page;
- consumer actions – such as purchasing of goods and services; and
- other internet behaviours – such as email, gaming and video streaming.

Because the demographic and other characteristics of panel members are known, it is possible to calculate the proportion of different types of people who visit individual websites or are exposed to banner advertising and how many times they are exposed in a given time period.

This is projected to the on-line population as a whole, enabling media planners and buyers to look at metrics that are comparable with other media – like 'Opportunities to See' banner advertising or reach and frequency.

A serious shortcoming of user-centric behaviour comes from the desire to measure internet usage at work – many corporations simply don't allow their employees to install non-approved software. Other usage outside the home (i.e. at internet cafes or universities) may also be missed or under-measured.

The other problem is that most sites are too small to generate a statistically robust audience from a panel. It is virtually impossible to build a sample size large enough to represent the browsing behaviour of every internet user with more than 33 billion individual web pages available.

The two major companies involved in user-centric measurement globally are Nielsen Online and comScore.

Nielsen Online

Nielsen's NetView service uses a desktop meter to identify which desktop or internet application is being used by the panellist's computer at any point in time and also includes a prompt in households where computers are shared, so that individual users can be monitored.

In May 2009, the service was offered in eleven countries: Australia, Brazil, France, Germany, Italy, Japan, Spain, Sweden, Switzerland, the UK and the USA.

The panels are recruited by telephone in order, the company says, to avoid the biases inherent in recruiting on-line (i.e. the probability that those responding to such an invitation on-line may be heavier internet users than the population as a whole or otherwise different).

Panel sizes vary - in the United States for example, 28,000 internet users are measured by Nielsen Online, enabling them to report audiences to around 3,000 individual sites. It was announced in 2009 that this number would increase to 200,000 during the year, raising the number of sites covered to an estimated 25,000.[20]

Even with a panel size this large, most internet sites will still be too small to be measured – or too small to carry out in-depth analysis on.

comScore

comScore's Media Metrix operates panels reporting both globally and for 37 individual countries. Its monthly reporting sample in the United States consists of 190,000 home users and 10,000 at work.[21]

Home users are defined as households where any user over 2 years of age has accessed the internet in the past 30 days – its work panel consists of adults aged 18 or over who have accessed the internet from an employer-owned computer in the previous 30 days. The size and characteristics of these universes are updated regularly through the company's continuous enumeration surveys.

Using its CProxy software agent, comScore tracks all digital activity and logs the sites visited by each panellist, capturing the content loaded onto the browser. Advertising exposure can be identified using either image matching (with known creative material) or by tagging ads in advance and logging receipt.

comScore uses a biometric or 'intelligent agent' technique it calls User Demographic Reporting (based on the pattern of keystrokes and mouse patterns) to identify specific individuals using shared computers on which its software is loaded. This, they argue, is preferable to continually asking people to verify their identity through pop-ups or other methods. Data is then weighted to the estimated universe of internet users before being published.

Tracking Through Portal

Downloading software in order to be measured, as panellists are asked to do by Nielsen Online and comScore, is not the only user-centric approach. Since 2004, internet audiences in the Netherlands have been measured using an approach known as 'Tracking Through Portal' (TTP).

On the Webmeter™ service, panelists access the internet through a start page, which identifies both the panelist and his point of access (e.g. home, work, school etc.). Because no software is downloaded to the user's computer, the challenges of measuring work and other Out of Home access is addressed. Multiple users of the same computer are identified by the login on the Webmeter start page.

The obvious challenge of such an approach is to ensure that panelists always log onto the start page before they surf the internet. To this end, various checks are made by the research vendors to ensure compliance.

As of June 2009, the Webmeter™ system tagged some 400 sites, with audiences to these sites tracked by a panel of 10,000 people.[22]

Network-centric measurement

Another approach to internet audience measurement is represented by companies like Hitwise, which monitors internet traffic volume represented by large numbers of users via anonymised data from Internet Service Providers (ISPs).

This allows them to overcome issues with small sample sizes that plague the user-centric approach, although they cannot identify the characteristics of users needed by advertisers.

So for example, some 10 million internet users in the United States are covered by Hitwise, enabling top-line audience counts to be delivered for relatively small websites not picked up by the user-centric panels.

The company can track the number of website visitors, how many pages they view and how long they spend on each page. An example of the kinds of analysis that can be carried out include:

- the ranking and market shares for individual websites within around 160 industry and market categories such as Search, healthcare, autos, financial and so on;
- intelligence on which websites are visited before and after specified sites or groups of sites, showing how users are being driven and routed between sites;
- deep dives into Search behaviour – for example looking at the incidence of Search terms according to the number of words typed into the search box (in April 2009, for example, it was reported that 20% of US search activity was based on typing in just a single word).[23]

Hitwise operates in the United States, Canada, Australia, New Zealand, Hong Kong, Singapore and the UK.

Hybrid measurement

Several companies, including Gemius, Nielsen Online and AGOF (Europe), Quantcast (the United States) and comScore (the USA, Canada and the UK) offer services which variously integrate on- and off-line research, site-centric and user-centric measurement to provide media sellers, planners and buyers with on-line media planning data.

As has been noted, cookie counts tend to inflate unique visitor numbers due to cookie deletion and multiple or shared machine usage. They also generate no information on the demographic characteristics of the audience. Panel data can only measure the largest sites.

Quantcast tags sites on behalf of web publishers and uses a model to build profiles of the individuals visiting the tagged sites. The two key adjustments they make to raw site-centric counts are (a) to translate the number of unique cookies downwards to a more realistic count of people and (b) to apply demographic and other descriptors to the counts unavailable from the site-centric data.

Their starting point is to recognise that, while raw cookie counts certainly inflate the number of people visiting websites, the extent of this is by no means equal across sites or over time.

To adjust the raw cookie data, Quantcast's model takes account of a number of factors which affect this adjustment[24] and apply them within their model:

- *Time period*: the shorter the period analysed, the less likely people are to visit a site, delete their cookie and re-visit the site;
- *Typical visit frequency*: some sites will be visited infrequently by most people, and therefore will not suffer unduly from cookie deletion. Others are visited more regularly and are more likely to see unique visitor counts inflated by cookie deletion over time;
- *Share of site usage from work or public machines*: some types of site are visited from both home and work computers; others are more likely only to be visited from home;
- *Types of site*: web portals like Google, MSN or Yahoo, are more likely than other kinds of site to have multiple people accessing them from the same machine.

To apply demographic and other characteristics to the user count, Quantcast uses a combination of data from tagged sites, market research companies, toolbar vendors and ISPs to infer the audience composition of measured sites.

comScore reported on a test of its methodology in Canada[25] where it tagged a range of websites so that all visits to the sites could be recorded (the 'site-centric' part of the measurement).

The surfing behaviour of its 30,000 panel of internet users was then combined with this information, adding demographic and unique visitor data to the raw numbers generated by the tagged sites.

The test showed that more than 10% of website visits came from outside Canada (and were therefore filtered out of the final results, alongside non-human and other traffic usually included in standard web server counts). A third of visits occurred during the working day – suggesting that much of it was taking place from the workplace.

Sites that were not tagged had audience estimates made through a special projection methodology based on findings from the sites that were tagged alongside the reported behaviour of panel members.

Hybrid measures offer the advantage that smaller sites can be measured beyond hits and page views, while the audiences to larger sites can be studied in greater depth. They will also reduce the confusion caused by the existence of two fundamentally different measurement techniques generating completely different audience numbers.

Engagement studies

Traditional media such as television, print, radio and Out of Home, as described in previous chapters, have moved beyond basic audience measurement in an attempt to show how people exposed to advertisements in their media are influenced.

Amongst the engagement measures they look at are time spent with their medium (e.g. with a magazine, programme or poster site), attentiveness to advertising and the role both the media and the advertising within it play in people's lives.

The larger website publishers are able to provide data on time spent with their sites and on specific web pages as part of their standard internet audience measurement reports. In addition, behaviour (such as how internet users move from site to site and whether or not they execute a purchase on-line) is also built into the basic audience metrics.

So to examine engagement beyond these kinds of measures some advertisers and website publishers have used survey-based approaches to uncover general insights into the role the internet plays in the lives of its users.

Marketing organisations working on behalf of internet companies have also conducted studies into the effectiveness of on-line advertising.

An example of this is a study carried out by the UK Internet Advertising Bureau in conjunction with media agency Carat into the small car category[26] in 2006. Using an on-line study of women in the target audience for small cars, it was found that the internet played an important role in people's search for car reviews and that an average of 20% of them were able to recognise each of the 15 on-line ads shown to them.

The study also showed that on-line advertising was the largest single communications driver of brand engagement in the category. Additional lessons were drawn on which formats and creative approaches worked most effectively.

Other unpublished brand engagement studies have been conducted by the IAB into a range of product categories including haircare, soft drinks and retail brands.

Dynamic Logic, a US-based research company, has developed what it calls a 'MarketNorms' database. This aggregates findings from several thousand internet advertising campaigns tracked by the company across multiple product categories. Results can be analysed in various ways according to demographics, the size and type of advertisement, the websites used, the product category and other factors that may contribute to brand lift.

A standard approach is used in the studies to allow for comparability across campaigns. A control group is recruited prior to a campaign starting and is compared with a similar sample recruited during and after the campaign has finished.

Typical measures collected from both samples include aided brand awareness, on-line advertising awareness, message association (between advertisement and brand), brand favourability and purchase intent. Results are compared between the two samples and analysis of the impact of the campaign on these measures is carried out.

In an analysis of the MarketNorms database carried out for the Online Publishers Association in July 2008, Dynamic Logic found that advertising on 'professional content sites' (i.e. those represented by the OPA) was more effective than the industry average. A follow-up study in January 2009 found this divergence to have increased.[27]

The basic message of the study was that environment matters; the content surrounding an ad is a more effective carrier of advertising when it is targeted and relevant to the target audience.

A report by Nielsen Online in April 2009[28] found that the trend towards introducing more video content and social networking content seemed to be improving the overall level of engagement with the internet medium.

According to the report, which compared audiences in February 2009 with those from six years previously, the number of unique users of on-line video destinations on a monthly basis rose more than three-fold (from a very small base) and actually surpassed the number accessing email sites in November 2007. Time spent on video sites grew almost twenty-fold.

These findings were echoed in the UK, where comScore reported in January 2009 that almost 30 million people had accessed on-line video (80% of internet users).

The Nielsen report went on to highlight the dramatic growth of social networking sites over recent years. Time spent on these sites also surpassed that spent on email in February 2009.

The future

A number of major issues remain for the internet medium as it continues its progress towards a more video-rich, interactive experience now used by the majority of the populations in the advanced industrial economies and growing rapidly everywhere.

The first is the inherent weaknesses of both the site-centric and user-centric approaches: the site-centric approach cannot identify individual users with sufficient accuracy for the marketer's purposes, while the user-centric approach cannot build large enough samples to measure the majority of sites. Hybrid approaches which seek to integrate these approaches in various ways are an important work in progress for the industry.

A second issue is how to assess the impact of consumers researching what they are looking to buy on-line, but making their actual purchases off-line. On-line commerce is growing in importance every year, but still remains small compared with purchasing in traditional retail outlets for most products and services.

One step in the direction of isolating the total return on investment from internet advertising was made in a joint study by comScore, MySpace and dunnhumby in early 2009.

Focusing on social network advertising expenditure,[29] the group set out to address the inherent challenge of identifying the impact of what is generally a small part of an overall marketing campaign. Because of this, it cannot usually be isolated within the market mix models used by many advertisers, tending to get 'lost' in what is termed 'statistical noise'.

The study was able to identify 60,000 individuals who were members of both dunnhumby's retailer loyalty card scheme in the United States and comScore's internet usage panel.

Dunnhumby compared purchasing of a brand advertising on MySpace between matched groups of consumers who had either been exposed or not exposed to the on-line campaign – concluding that the brand in question had generated off-line sales valued in excess of its on-line advertising investment.

A third issue becoming increasingly important is the whole area of user privacy. Regulators in the European Union and the United States, for example, have expressed concern over the use of techniques such as Deep Packet Inspection (which governments also use to ensure web users are complying with the law).[30]

Deep Packet Inspection allows telecoms network operators to examine the content of data packets moving through the internet. By evaluating the content an individual searches for and receives, the technology can be used to build detailed profiles of these individuals which, in turn, can be used to target them with ad messages and other content to which they are expected to be more receptive.

A fourth challenge for the internet industry is to develop a richer set of measures to encompass the very different advertising environments available. For example, as the popularity of social networking sites grows, measures need to be developed which help advertisers gain a fuller impression of the depth and breadth of conversations being carried on within these sites.[31] This will be about more than hits and clicks.

Ideally, a marketer will want to know whether comments about their brands or services are negative, positive or neutral. How do conversations about brands evolve over time? And how, if at all, do they spread?

Is the internet doomed to be simply a direct response medium, with its success gauged purely by the number of visitors, click-thrus and measured actions?

Google in the UK set out to investigate whether Search advertising – the ultimate measurable medium – could actually be shown to have a broader impact on softer brand health measures like consumer attitudes.[32] As with the social networking example above, they were faced with the problem that even Search, the largest component of internet advertising, is too small to register in most marketing mix models.

To address this, the research partner recruited a sample directly from the websites running a selected campaign to ensure they spoke to people likely to have been exposed to the advertising being tested (which could be identified using their cookies) and asked a series of brand attitude questions. These were combined with other questions on people's recall and recognition of certain images from the campaign as well as their past experience with the brand. Following a two-stage modelling process, they were able to conclude that Search advertising did, in this case, have a measurable positive influence on consumer engagement with the brand.

Internet audience measurement is a fast-moving target. No doubt by the time this book is published, much will have changed or developed. The move away from looking only at site-centric or panel-centric measurement and instead finding ways to bring them together will be the key challenge of the next few years.

7 Measuring mobile media

Like web analytics, mobile analytics is hard.

Eric T. Peterson[1]

Introduction

At the end of 2008, there were estimated to be some 3 billion mobile phone subscribers globally, holding a total of 4.1 billion mobile phone accounts (many people having more than one phone). The number of subscriptions is equivalent to 61 out of every 100 people in the world.

This is more than twice the number of internet subscribers, paid-for newspaper readers or credit card holders and more than three times the number of landline telephones.[2] See Table 7.1 for details.

According to one source, more mobile phones have built-in cameras than all the cameras ever made and more phones equipped to play music are sold than iPods.[3]

Total industry revenues (hardware and services combined) exceeded $1 trillion in 2008.

Unlike the internet, which has been slow to spread to the developing world, mobile phones reached the equivalent of 40% of the developing world's population at the end of 2007;[4] it has reached virtual saturation in advanced industrial nations.

Mainly this is because of the relative ease and cheapness with which a mobile phone network can be built compared with the infrastructure needed for a landline system of communication.

It also opens up the potential for the 'seventh medium' (after television, cinema, print, radio, posters and the internet) to be the first truly global mass medium, available to all people in all countries, free from the limitations imposed by economics and literacy.

Table 7.1 Global Information & Communication Technologies snapshot, 2008

Technology	Number per 100 inhabitants
Mobile cellular subscriptions	61.1
Internet users	23.0
Fixed telephone lines	18.9
Fixed broadband subscribers	6.1
Mobile broadband subscriptions	5.0
Read paid-for newspapers	28.0

Source: ITU World Telecommunication/ICT Indicators Database; World Association of Newspapers

In 2001 a technology known as 3G (for Third Generation) was launched in Japan. This superseded 2G, primarily designed for voice and text messaging, by enabling users to transmit and receive greater amounts of data on their phones – giving them the ability to access the internet, swap photo and video messages and more.

Today, an estimated 400 million people can access this technology;[5] yet 20 years ago almost nobody carried a phone with them, let alone used it to watch television, surf the internet, create and share photos or video, send and receive emails, search for nearby movie theatres or listen to their favourite song.

A brief history of mobile phones

Although the very earliest mobile phones were pioneered in the 1940s, it was on 3 April 1973, that a researcher for Motorola, Marty Cooper, made the first call on a hand-held mobile phone. A press conference had been held at the Hilton hotel in New York that day to introduce the device.

Cooper then decided to step outside into the street and make a call in front of a journalist and several passers by, reportedly almost getting knocked over by a car in the process, but inaugurating the first big step towards person-to-person, rather than place-to-place communication. He was said to have been inspired by watching Captain Kirk from *Star Trek* making calls on his communicator.[6]

The first mobile phone network based on cellular technology was launched in Japan in 1979, followed by systems in the Nordic countries and Denmark in 1981.

But it was Bell Laboratories which, in 1984, succeeded in developing the cellular technology that would drive commercial adoption of mobile phones. The basic idea behind cellular networks is that certain geographical areas (or cells) are covered by centrally controlled and partially overlapping 'base stations' which transmit and receive calls. People carrying phones can move between and amongst the sites covered by each base station without losing their signal using a technology known as 'handover' or 'handoff'.

Then there were the phones themselves. The Motorola DynaTAC 8000X was the world's first commercial handheld cellular phone. It allowed its user to speak for up to 30 minutes, could go 8 hours between charges, measured 33 × 9 centimetres and weighed almost a kilogram. The phone also took 10 hours to recharge. Most impressively, it was priced at just under $4,000!

Digital cellular phones (2G) were introduced in 1991 in Finland, the country that also pioneered the first text messaging service two years later. The move from analogue to digital communication allowed for a better user experience – more calls could be carried on within individual cells, while the way was opened up for inherently digital services like text messaging and internet access.

By the mid-1990s, mobile phones had become smaller, lighter and more fashionable looking – the Motorola StarTAC, for example, was introduced in January 1996 weighing in at just 88 grams and costing a mere $1,000.

But the bandwidth offered by the 2G networks for adding data services was limited, making the user experience less than satisfactory. Once the possibility was introduced for making the mobile phone not just a phone, but also an organiser, a camera, a text and photo messaging system, an internet browser, an email device and a television set, faster broadband data speeds were needed. So in 2001, as noted above, the first 3G phone networks and handsets entered the scene.

By the end of 2008, following very substantial investments by mobile phone network providers, around 400 million 3G subscriptions had been taken out, with Japan and South Korea leading the world at around 67 subscriptions per 100 inhabitants, followed by Singapore (61), Australia (53) and Italy (48).[7]

Larger markets like the USA had around 20 3G subscriptions per 100 inhabitants, while the UK had 32.

To take account of the growing range of capabilities opened up by faster communication speeds, IBM put the first 'smartphone', the Simon, on sale in 1993. It contained a calendar, address book, calculator and a world clock. It could send and receive emails, while users could play games, all from a touch-screen interface.

A number of other models were introduced in the years that followed, including the Blackberry in 2001. Each was more sophisticated than the last, culminating in the launch of Apple's iPhone in 2007. By the end of 2008, almost 200 different mobile phone models were on sale in the US market alone.

The iPhone, like its growing number of competitors, offers email and internet browsing, a portable media player and an in-built camera. It also features around 100,000 mini-programmes or 'apps' built by third-party developers offering users games, currency converters, calorie trackers, books, maps, ringtones and just about anything else they can come up with. Users can download these applications for free or for a nominal price.

Smartphone apps are likely to be major drivers of brand preference. As of June 2009, Apple's total was almost ten times that of its nearest competitor Google's Android, although Google is now racing to catch up.[8]

Asia has led the world almost from the start in the development and usage of mobile technologies. In May 2009, a study by TNS[9] reported that almost a third of consumers in Japan, South Korea and Hong Kong had used their mobile phones to watch television, compared with just 8% in Europe and 11% in the United States. Mobile TV functions were considered to be a key driver when choosing a new handset in these countries.

In the United States, a study in early 2009[10] found that 51% of mobile phone users accessed content on their phones every week, spending about the same amount of time on the task as they did on phone calls or sending texts. Those not using the data facilities on their phones tended to be put off by the price of access.

Mobile usage today

There is no doubt that, as the user experience improves through better handsets and faster network speeds, people are going to spend more time doing more things with their mobile phones than simply talking and texting.

Take surfing the internet. A study by Ipsos Reid in Canada, for example, found that one out of six on-line Canadians who owned a mobile phone spent almost an hour accessing the internet every day.[11]

comScore[12] in the United States in January 2009 reported that 63 million mobile phone users looked at news and information monthly, of which 22.4 million did so daily. Other popular activities on a daily basis included accessing social networking sites (9.3 million), entertainment information (5.5 million) and movie information (3 million).

Many are also using their phones to watch short or even long-form video. Nielsen's 'Three Screen Report'[13] for the first quarter of 2009 showed that in the United States, while viewing of video on either the internet or mobile phone was growing, it has a long way to go before it catches up with television.

The average American, according to the study, watches about 153 hours of television every month at home. 131 million of them watch video on the internet for an average of about 3 hours each month at home and work. The 13.4 million people who have watched video on their mobile phones see on average about 3½ hours of mobile video each month.

Once account is taken of the fact that only a small (but growing) minority of people actually watch video on their phones, it amounts to less than 1% of all video viewing taking place.

However, one noteworthy fact which comes out in this and other studies is that younger, teenage consumers watch almost twice as much video on their phones as the average adult – and tend to watch more video on their mobile phones than they do on the internet. It remains to be seen whether these behaviours will stay with them as they grow older.

Another development is the use of mobile phones as a way of accessing instant information about products and services. Google announced in May 2009, for example, that users of its Android smartphone could download an application free which allows them to scan barcodes in retail stores to compare the price the item is retailing for on-line. An iPhone app, Snaptell, also provides product reviews and price comparisons for certain types of product.

Games are also proving popular, especially in parts of Asia such as South Korea, where the quality of games is becoming higher and higher.

This popularity is driven by several factors including the high penetration of 3G, higher quality handsets, lower prices and an emphasis on high-quality products.

To maintain quality in South Korea for example, a panel of mobile games testers try out each game before it is released onto an operator's portal – games usually have to go through this process several times before they pass. According to Screen Digest,[14] a sample of best-selling UK mobile games was put through this test and almost all failed to pass.

Advertising on mobile phones

As a medium, mobile offers a number of advantages to advertisers including:

- a built-in payment mechanism – subscribers pay for whatever they do via their monthly phone bills or pre-paid credits;
- it is uniquely personal – computers, newspapers, the television screen, the radio and other media can be shared by other users. The mobile phone is likely to be used only by one person or household unit;
- it is often carried throughout the day and even left on at night – meaning the phone is always likely to be where the person owning it happens to be;
- it offers the potential for highly accurate audience measurement – usage can be tracked in great detail by the network carrier, unhindered by cookies, firewalls or viewing away from the device.

Estimates of the size of the mobile advertising market differ considerably depending on the source consulted. Gartner, for example, calculated that global mobile adspend would hit around $2.7 billion in 2008 (around 0.6% of global adspend in that year), up from $1.7 billion in 2007.[15] There are considerable variations in estimates at the individual market level as well (which do not come close to matching Gartner's global estimate).

In the UK, for example, official estimates from the Internet Advertising Bureau put the size of the market in 2008 at £28.6 million (US$46m) – twice as high as spending the previous year. The growth was driven by increasing numbers of mobile web users, a better user experience, a mushrooming in the number of participants in mobile social networks and a greater professionalism in the industry.

In Europe, Vodafone Media Solutions valued the mobile marketplace at around €149 million.[16]

The Kelsey Group estimated US mobile ad spending at $160 million in 2008,[17] a number expected to double in 2009.

Forecasts for the global marketplace over the next few years span a wide range of possibilities ranging from $8 billion to $24 billion by 2013.

Components of mobile advertising include:

- *Text messaging*: sending alerts, offers, coupons or information direct to consumers.
- *Mobile search*: Just as they can on their PCs and laptops, mobile phone subscribers can search for information on their phones using dedicated, mobile-friendly search engines. Advertisers can pay to feature near the top of these searches based on the words used. An advantage offered by the mobile device as a search tool is that it can often be localised to the geographical area where the search is being carried out due to GPS tracking of the phone's location. For the owner of a local restaurant, therefore, a special offer could be transmitted to a potential customer in the vicinity looking for somewhere to eat.
- *Display*: Again, just as advertisers can purchase banner ads on the internet, so too banner ads and other forms of messaging can be featured on the pages looked at by mobile users as they surf the web, play games, participate in social networking or watch video clips. Video is often offered free in return for consumers agreeing to view advertising. Within text messages, links to ads are also sometimes featured which are included within the display category.

As with other media, the likelihood of a consumer being exposed to advertising is partly dependent on what sorts of content they seek and how often they look at it. The possibilities are as wide as the internet, although not all websites have been re-purposed to fit the smaller screens on a mobile device.

The *New York Times*, for example, offers an application built for the iPhone, a text messaging service for delivering news and a dedicated mobile site which users can browse, search or complete the crossword on. All the content can be accessed for free or at a nominal price and is supported by advertising.

The number of mobile users streaming or downloading video content is growing, as broadband speeds increase and the programming on offer improves. Much of the content is supported by so-called 'pre-roll' advertising, which plays before the video starts.

Marketers can use mobile advertising to build databases of customers according to how they respond to their various offers – with the advantage that, unlike with other media, they can be pretty sure of reaching specific individuals every time, once they have their phone numbers. Users can be incentivised with loyalty schemes, special offers and mobile coupons for agreeing to be part of a customer database.

Indeed mobile phone users leave a trail of data behind them that can be exploited for marketing purposes including where they are, how much they use the phone, what they use it for and how much they spend on their subscription.

The highly personal nature of mobile offers both advantages and all the attendant sensibilities of talking directly to people in a way they find difficult to avoid. With more advanced, GPS-equipped phones, it is possible to reach people when they are situated at specific locations – e.g. near a restaurant or store – and to target them with offers and incentives relevant to their location.

Consumer acceptance of advertising

Countless studies appear on almost a daily basis about mobile usage and behaviour. Because of the fast-changing nature of the mobile environment, many are dated almost as soon as they appear. Nevertheless, to pick just a few from mid-2009:

- A report from GfK and Brightkite covering 1,000 US mobile phone users reported that, in the first quarter of 2009, 38% of US mobile subscribers recalled seeing mobile advertising on their mobile phones, although the number rose to 59% of smartphone users; 23% of smartphone users recalled seeing text messaging ads, 28% recalled mobile web ads and 15% had seen ads within video material.
- A survey commissioned by Orange in the UK in March 2009 found that two-thirds of the 2,000 respondents contacted (across

all mobile networks) had used short SMS codes (abbreviated SMS text numbers used on print advertising, TV and radio advertising, on marketing promotional literature, on-pack marketing and on outdoor advertising; they can be used by consumers to respond to promotions, receive mobile coupons or take part in polls; a particularly popular one has been a code which allows people to take a companion free to see the movies on Wednesdays).

- KPMG's third annual Global Consumers and Convergence survey of more than 4,000 people in 19 countries was released in March 2009. It found that 29% of mobile phone users surveyed in the USA were willing to see advertising in return for free songs. Globally, 49% of consumers would accept ads on their mobile phones in return for songs.

But despite all the optimism shown in the many studies published on advertising acceptance and usage by consumers, the medium is still inhibited to some extent by platform issues. The multiplicity of mobile phone designs and configurations and different user interfaces complicates the task of creating ads that work equally well on all handsets. It also complicates the measurement task.

There are varying schools of thought on how best the mobile medium can be used. Is it better as a direct response mechanism, taking advantage of its ability to contextualise messages to specific locations? Or is it more effective as a simple branding device given its ability to reach people anytime, anywhere with a high likelihood that they will see the advertising sent to them?

And will consumers tolerate this very personal device being hijacked by advertisers for their own purposes? It is easy to find examples of consumer irritation with what they consider irrelevant or invasive text advertising. It is equally easy to find commercially sponsored studies which accentuate the positive consumer attitudes to advertising on their mobile devices.

Governments and regulatory authorities are already studying how to protect consumer privacy on the internet with possible negative effects for advertisers. This is also an issue – perhaps an even greater one – for mobile devices. To date it is too early to say how the optimum level will be found.

Audience measurement

In the same way that many people find advertising on their mobile phones to be an invasion of their privacy – something they do not find to be such an issue in the traditional media or on-line – they may also find the idea of having their behaviour tracked without their knowledge to be a worrisome thought.

But of course people's usage of their mobile phone, to a far greater extent than their usage of the internet, can be quite precisely tracked. All mobile devices need a Subscriber Identity Module or SIM card and a telephone number associated with it. In most cases, these numbers can be matched with a name, address and credit card details by a network operator.

Mobile phone operators know which numbers they call or text, what content they download, how long they spend on the phone and where they are when the phone is switched on (although they cannot always monitor what users do when they are not connected to the network – for example listening to music or playing games). Unlike on the internet, individuals cannot easily hide behind multiple browsers or devices or delete cookies to cover their tracks.

Due to privacy concerns, these data are not being used in the way they could be used – but the potential exists, at the very least, for de-personalised versions of the information to be exploited by marketers.

The effectiveness of a mobile ad campaign is currently measured in various ways. The main approaches, as with the internet, include site-centric metrics such as impressions (views), click-through rates and conversion rates and user-centric metrics such as claimed behaviour, decision drivers and recall of advertising. The latter also enables advertisers to look at demographic information.

A good example of the many ways in which the mobile consumer can be measured is offered by US audience provider Nielsen Online, which categorises its mobile audience measurement service under three broad headings: consumer behaviour, consumer experience and consumer attitudes.

Consumer behaviour measurement encompasses three different services:

- The *Mobile Network Signal Poll.* This reports the market shares of the various mobile network operators in 65 key US metro markets every month (and 100 further markets on a less frequent basis) through automatically and passively polling large samples of telephone numbers to verify which operators control the numbers.

- The *On-line Bill Panel*. A sample of around 35,000 people who have agreed to have their phone bills monitored allows Nielsen to automatically capture and record the bills on-line, without the need for them to do anything. Analysis can then be carried out on the entire database or sub-sections of it against the various items recorded on the bills – e.g. the size of the bill, the share of long-distance versus international calls, the types of ringtones downloaded and so on.
- The *Meter Panel*. Although not yet in operation (at the time of writing in early 2009), Nielsen plans to embed meters into smartphones at the manufacturing stage (to be activated only with the permission of subscribers). It will measure every interaction users have with their mobile phones, enabling analyses to be carried out into behaviours including the websites they visit, the games they play, the texts they receive and the advertising they are exposed to.

Consumer experience is measured using two methods:

- The *Mobile Network Testing Fleet*. Using specially equipped lorries which travel the length and breadth of the United States, this service tests the signal quality of every network in every US market once a year (twice a year in the largest markets). Companies can use it, for example, to compare customer satisfaction and disconnection behaviour with signal quality.
- *Application Testing Nodes*. Installed in more than 20 US cities, the testing nodes measure how well mobile networks and devices perform for a range of applications including speed of internet access, the time taken for photo messages to move between one city and another, VOIP applications and mobile television quality. The tests are carried out around the clock, allowing identification and analysis of the consumer experience.

Consumer attitudes are measured via on-line and off-line surveys of various kinds. Competitor comScore offers three main audience measurement services: MobiLens, Mobile Metrix and Ad Metrix Mobile.

- MobiLens is a syndicated on-line monthly survey used to capture all kinds of usage of the mobile phone including information about the device, the data services used and the media consumption and demographic characteristics of around 40,000 users in the USA, the UK, Germany, France, Spain and Italy.
- Mobile Metrix is a meter integrated into around 4,000 smartphones which captures mobile internet surfing behaviour and media consumption in the USA and the UK.
- Ad Metrix Mobile identifies which advertisers are running mobile display campaigns, where they are running these campaigns and which ad servers are delivering the advertisements.

Mobile advertising networks

Mobile advertising networks like Admob, which serves over 7 billion ads for more than 7,000 mobile websites, offers advertisers data on the number of page views, time spent on each page and so-called 'bounce rates' (i.e. the number of visitors who visit only one page within a site before moving onto other sites) aggregated from the sites that use their technologies.

The company releases a monthly Mobile Metrics Report summarising key data from their ad requests. These can be broken down by country, by operating system, by handset model and by network operator. In its April 2009 report, for example, it found that smartphone users were far more likely than non-users to browse the web.

Gartner's reported share for smartphones against total device sales in 2008 (12%) was compared with Admob's worldwide ad requests – 35% of which originated from smartphones in April 2009. iPhone's operating system had an 8% share of the smartphone marketplace but generated 43% of all mobile web requests.[18]

Mobile web analytics

Various approaches are employed to measure mobile web surfing, although none are able to provide a comprehensive view of activity across all types of device. For example tracking mobile web usage through cookies is not supported by all mobile devices and will miss a large part of the audience. Even where they are supported, cookies are often cleared automatically between browsing sessions to save memory.

The JavaScript tagging of individual web pages is also not supported by all mobile devices or browsers and so will again only provide a partial view of the audience.

As a result, mobile analytics reports typically break down results by device type, platform and network operator. As with web analytics – for those devices where data is reported – detailed information can be gleaned about how many visitors each page attracts and the journeys they take to and from the page.

For advanced smartphones like the iPhone and Nokia's N95, which accept browser cookies and run JavaScript, mobile analytics is relatively straightforward – they also provide a better user experience and so encourage greater activity – which explains the results of Admob's survey.

But the wide variety of mobile browsers, devices and networks and their varying age and sophistication all add to the difficulty of collecting audience data to any given advertisement or site. Mobile web counts also suffer from some of the issues plaguing the internet, such as the activities of robots and other automated requests that cannot be attributed to an individual.

The missing piece

Companies like Admob and Bango can provide mobile advertisers with very rich data about the performance of their ads – but only through the sites on which their technology is present.

The missing piece in much of the current mobile audience measurement puzzle has been data from the mobile network operators, who have been wary of releasing data on their subscribers to third parties in case they fall foul of privacy laws in various countries. As is the case with the internet ISPs, it is ultimately these network providers who hold the key to accurate, comprehensive and granular data on mobile phone usage.

In February 2009 the GSMA, an organisation representing the mobile communications industry, announced the results of a survey[19] looking at the audience to 167,648 mobile websites according to the number of visitors, the number of page impressions and the time and duration of visits. Carried out in the UK, the survey was based on a sample of anonymous data from wireless carriers and showed that the operators' own carrier sites captured some 68% of visits to mobile sites in December

2008. Google sites ranked second, followed by Facebook – which was the leading site measured by time spent browsing.

The survey was carried out as part of a feasibility study into how best to create a measurement system for mobile browsing which will respect the privacy of mobile consumers. The GSMA in conjunction with the main mobile phone network operators plans to roll out a full audience measurement service in the UK in late 2009.

In the United States, the Mobile Marketing Association has released a set of audience definitions[20] against which they hope to see measurement services develop in the coming years. They are based on similar definitions developed for the internet in 2004. The four key definitions outline how ad impressions, streamed video advertising, rich media and clicks should be measured. Emphasis is placed on the user actually receiving the ad message, rather than it having simply been sent.

The future

It is early days in both the usage of mobile as an advertising medium and in its audience measurement. As a result, only a sketch of some of the audience measurement techniques currently available can be attempted. All have strengths and weaknesses.

However, mobile offers the potential to be one of the most measurable of media. Steps have now been taken to bring the network operators into the heart of the measurement system to reveal data on network traffic – the site-centric part of the audience measurement equation. Companies like Nielsen Online, comScore and others plan to continue their own efforts to provide both user-centric measurement and other information on the mobile phone audience.

As the quality of the data from mobile devices improves, it will be important to somehow link the audience information generated by them with data from the internet as, at the end of the day, the same people are accessing content through different platforms. From the point of view of the marketer, they are all consumers and potential customers. Which brings us neatly to the question of how we can look at the audiences to all of the media examined in these chapters.

8 Integrating media audience measurement

Introduction

Over the course of the previous chapters we have seen how audiences are measured to magazines, newspapers, television, radio, posters, the internet and mobile. The common factor is, of course, the audience.

The same people watch television, read newspapers and magazines, listen to the radio, surf the internet, and travel past posters. Sometimes they take part in more than one of these activities at the same time.

Marketers want to reach these people with their messages because they are all consumers. Ideally they would like to reach the people most likely to be receptive to their messages, whenever and however they can. So they, like consumers themselves, are 'media-neutral'.

This is not true for audience measurement services. Historically, each medium has been looked at separately and differently. The very definition of the 'audience' to commercials or content varies both by country and by medium.

For example, somebody is counted as a member of the television audience – broadly speaking – when they are in the room with a television set switched on and they register their presence by means of pressing a button on their peoplemeter. Their presence can then be matched, minute by minute, with what is showing on the screen at the time.

People are counted as being in the audience to a magazine or newspaper if they can remember reading or looking through any issue of a given title within its publication period. In most cases, no account is taken of which specific issues, let alone which pages or particular content they may have seen.

The audience to an internet or mobile web page can be measured in various ways, ranging from a count of how many 'unique cookies' are visiting the page to the proportion of a metered panel that see it.

And the audience to a roadside poster, depending on the country, can be as simple as a count of the number of people driving past the site or as complex as a visibility-adjusted estimate of the number of people likely to see it as they walk or drive by.

Audience measurement has evolved separately for each medium for many reasons. Print audience measurement, which developed in the 1930s and 1940s, was never going to adopt the household-based electronic measurement system television and radio were able to develop early on in the United States, because people read in many places and (until recently) did not have to switch their publication on to read it.

Radio had to drop its early meter as people started to listen out of the home – the research method had to follow the listeners.

It also made sense for the internet and mobile media to make full use of their in-built measurement characteristics from the beginning.

More recently, the fact that the bulk of funding for audience measurement has come from the media means that the shape of the services developed has tended to follow the interests of individual media, rather than the wider interest of advertisers and media agencies.

All this said, there remains a demand for information on how people use the whole range of different media available to them. Advertisers want to target their most receptive prospects across all the media they use. They also want to be able to make decisions about how to optimise scarce marketing budgets between the available options.

Media marketing organisation studies

Around the world, it is common for the marketing bodies representing individual media to commission multi-media studies that demonstrate the relative power and influence of their own particular medium versus other media.

So as discussed in previous chapters, the radio industry has commissioned multiple studies over the years showing how adding radio to a television campaign can reach otherwise un-reached consumers with a message, as well as adding depth and breadth to it.

Magazine and newspaper marketing bodies have published similar materials over the years – usually, as with their radio brethren, targeted against advertisers focused exclusively or mainly on television.

Aside from these efforts, several broad approaches have been developed to address the need for multi-media campaign reach and frequency information.

Syndicated single-source research

These attempt to capture all the data needed on a single survey. A good example of this kind of approach is the Target Group Index (TGI) which offers subscribers in 67 countries information on media consumption, product and brand usage and consumer attitudes.[1]

Launched in the UK in 1969, the survey generally takes the form of a substantial questionnaire, mailed or placed with a representative sample of adults, which they fill in and return to the research organisation.

Advertisers and their agencies can use the survey to identify the brand preferences of particular groups of consumers – e.g. people who have purchased dog food in the past four weeks. They can then look at how this same group of people view television, read magazines and newspapers, listen to the radio and surf the internet.

The data is not available at the same level of detail provided by the industry 'currency' surveys detailed in previous chapters. Indeed it cannot be, as many respondents would baulk at an even longer survey than the one they are already being asked to fill in (it may take 2–3 hours to diligently fill in a TGI questionnaire).

The TGI is not the only survey of its kind. Many mainstream readership surveys, such as the EGM study, which operates across ten Latin American countries, the US MRI survey or the UK's National Readership Survey, collect data on media usage that goes beyond the publications they are primarily designed to measure.

MRI, in fact, places a separate questionnaire about product usage with respondents after they have completed a face-to-face survey on readership, to avoid 'contaminating' the readership results.

The fundamental limitation of syndicated single-source surveys is, in short, that they have to try to cover every major product category and every medium within a single questionnaire. For this reason, the data they can provide on any given product category or medium is necessarily limited.

The Eurisko Media Monitor (EMM) – described briefly in Chapter 4 attempted to overcome the respondent burden by capturing part of the multi-media data 'passively' in Italy.[2] Technically, the device is able to monitor television viewing and radio listening via picking up specially encoded audio signals transmitted by participating stations, without the respondent having to do anything but carry the device with them. In addition, the portable meter is equipped with a barcode scanner and voice recorder, enabling respondents to record magazine and newspaper reading.

The EMM was trialled in 2006 and 2007 on a combined sample of 4,600 individuals. Each respondent was asked to carry the meter for a period of four weeks; they were also visited weekly by interviewers to verify their previous week's exposure to print, cinema and internet usage. Prior to this, they were interviewed face-to-face and asked about themselves, their brand and product consumption and their internet and cinema behaviour.

A challenge of such an all-encompassing survey is to monitor compliance with the tasks required. A motion sensor on the meter verifies whether or not the device is carried around all day, while the interviewer was able to discuss each week's compliance directly with the respondent on her visits.

The burden on respondents was heavy – they were being asked to carry the meter all the time, scan in their reading of newspapers and magazines and also any cinema visits or surfing of the internet. They also had to make time to see the interviewer every week for a month.

This added appreciably to the cost of the study, as well as placing question marks on the representativeness of interviewees and the veracity of their scanning behaviour. In addition, the task of integrating the different kinds of information generated by the research (e.g. audio matching data, interview results, scanning data etc.) was not insubstantial.

Drawing from the lessons of these early studies, the third wave of the Eurisko study commenced in February 2009 with a larger sample and greater continuity of fieldwork. Coverage was extended to include visits to major retail outlets, time spent out of the home and exposure to ads in train stations and airports.

Most significantly, the weekly interviewer visits were replaced with a new device – the Eurisko Dialogue Machine – enabling panellists to complete short daily surveys themselves on print, internet and outdoor media exposure alongside weekly surveys about retail and cinema visits.

Single source research, whether it consists of lengthy surveys or a combination of methods such as the Eurisko approach, inevitably places heavy burdens on respondents. Issues such as response and compliance are key to making such research a valid representation of multi-media consumption. It will be interesting to see to what extent the results of the 2009 Eurisko survey match audience estimates generated by existing single media surveys in the Italian marketplace.

It is also worth mentioning yet another single source experiment carried out in the United States, Project Apollo. In early 2006, following several months of development and piloting, around 5,000 households on Nielsen's Homescan panel (a panel where participants are asked to record all their grocery purchases using portable scanners) were also equipped with Arbitron's Portable Peoplemeter device so their media exposure could be simultaneously tracked.

The idea behind the initiative was to examine the extent to which advertising exposure could be linked to brand buying behaviour from the same group of people.

The project, however, proved to be financially unviable and was abandoned in February 2008, although those who saw the data found it to have been useful.

Another US service, TRA, combines set-top box tuning data with frequent shopper card data from a number of retailers to offer a panel of around 375,000 homes where the two data streams can be linked.

Custom single-source surveys

An approach which has gained popularity with some marketers in recent years is to carry out custom surveys targeting only the consumers considered to be 'in the market' for a particular product and to focus on the individual media considered relevant to the product.

One company that has developed a service of this kind is Integration, with its Market ContactAudit® approach.[3] Broadly-speaking, this involves an advertiser selecting a target audience of interest to them (e.g. people who have bought within their product category recently or plan to do so shortly).

A series of focus groups are tapped to assist the marketer in drawing up a list of all the main types of influence on their purchase within the product category in question – which can range from traditional advertising-supported media to other consumer touchpoints such as word of mouth or the advice they receive from sales staff. These are then presented to a larger sample of respondents who are asked a series of questions which help determine the relative strength of each touchpoint on their brand choice. Survey responses are then used to create recommendations on the appropriate marketing mix the brand should consider.

Other custom multi-media solutions are offered by companies like Millward Brown, whose Demand & Activation approach also seeks to gauge the relative strength of different consumer influences and make recommendations on the right mix of media for a brand.

These approaches have strengths and weaknesses. But they are not 'currency' surveys; they may suggest that newspapers or television should be used to promote a brand, but they will not recommend which newspapers, channels or times of day should be employed. There is also debate as to whether it is really possible to ask people in surveys about which media are most influential on them.

Data fusion

A third approach is to try to join together existing surveys using complex mathematical techniques. The basic idea is that any two (or more) surveys will have data they collect in common from their respondents, such as demographics (sex, age, income, location etc.) and perhaps other general media consumption information.

It is then possible to take information from a respondent on one survey and 'fuse' it onto one or more similar respondents on other surveys, thereby enabling information from both surveys to be used from a single database. There is much controversy over even the theory of doing this and plenty of debate over the various mathematical techniques used to carry out the fusion.

But despite the controversy it is now fairly common practice in Europe and increasingly in North America to do just this, enabling media planners to paint a picture of multi-media consumption that links directly back to the surveys used to carry out detailed planning in individual media.

Hub and fusion

Taking a step beyond basic data fusion, the Institute of Practitioners in Advertising in the UK decided, after consultation with the industry, to embark on their Touchpoints survey. The idea was first to produce what they refer to as a 'hub' survey, onto which each of the single-medium currency surveys would then be fused.

Two studies have been carried out to date. In the second, a group of 5,465 respondents were asked in late 2007 to fill in a detailed questionnaire covering their media usage, shopping behaviour and lifestyles. They were then asked to carry a PDA with them over the course of seven days, using it to indicate, half hour by half hour, the activities they were involved in at the time – including any media they might be exposed to and the mood they were in.

Planners can access the hub data, covering people's media consumption by time of day (not previously available for media like print and Out of Home). They can then link the insights derived from this to detailed media planning recommendations using the Integrated database. So a planner may be able to look at the best mix of media for reaching people say, on the day before they go shopping. Or a publisher might look at how best to promote the Saturday edition of its newspaper against readers of competitive titles. The Touchpoints approach has been emulated in several countries including France and Poland and many others have been examining it with interest.

Summary

Many attempts have been made to provide multi-media research to help marketers and media agency planners to make sense of the whole gamut of consumer behaviour, with respect both to the brands they buy and the media they are exposed to.

As media companies 'converge', distributing the content they create across multiple platforms, the financial imperative to design and execute audience measurement that captures the totality of consumer media behaviour is likely to increase. Many television stations and publishers for example, are re-defining themselves as 'content creators'. They operate in their traditional domains, but also offer websites, podcasts, mobile applications and discussion forums for users to feed back to them.

As a result, they need to understand whether these different platforms are bringing them new readers and viewers, or whether they are simply providing alternative ways for their traditional customers to access content. Marketers will look to them to provide detailed information on how many and what kind of people will have the opportunity to see their messages across multiple platforms. As has been seen, the different ways in which people use media on these platforms will need to be understood, while the gap between the various ways in which audiences have traditionally been defined and measured on single-medium currency surveys will have to be bridged.

Much useful work is being carried out, as described above. Over the next few years the integration of different types of information, whether collected from devices (site-centric internet and mobile data, set-top box tuning data, automatic traffic counts) or people (panels, surveys, passive monitoring devices) will be the key challenge for the audience measurement business.

Notes

Chapter 1: Introduction

1 *Why Fifa's claim of one billion TV viewers was a quarter right.* The Independent, 1 March 2007.
2 Advertising Research Foundation (2003). *Making Better Media Decisions.* New York.
3 Narayanan, Arvind and Shmatikov, Vitaly (2009). *De-anonymizing Social Networks.* University of Texas at Austin. http://randomwalker.info/social-networks/index.html

Chapter 2: Measuring print media

1 Haentzschel, Carl Alexander (2007). *News Flows in Singapore.* Doctoral thesis. http://edoc.hu-berlin.de/dissertationen/haentzschel-carl-alexander-2007-08-22/PDF/haentzschel.pdf
2 http://www.wan-press.org/article6476.html
3 World Association of Newspapers (2009). *World Press Trends.* http://www.bnet.com/2407-13071_23-305546.html
4 Magazine Publishers Association (15 June 2009) *2009/10 Magazine Handbook.* http://www.magazine.org/news/index.aspx
5 Brown, Michael (1994). *Lies, Damned Lies and Replication.* Admap, April 1994.
6 Brown, Michael (1999). *Effective Print Media Measurement.* http://www.readershipsymposium.org/node/2361
7 *Summary of Current Readership Research.* E. Meier, Proceedings of the 13th Worldwide Readership Symposium, Vienna, October 2007.
8 Corlett, Tom (1989). *JICNARS and NRS: The Historical Perspective.* Admap, December 1989.
9 Henry, Harry (1991). *Origins and Birth of the NRS.* Admap, September 1991.
10 Henry, Harry (1991). *Ibid.*
11 Meier, Erhard (1995). *The Fabulous Paradox of the NRS.* Admap, July 1995.
12 Banick, Douglas (1981). *Magazine Audience Measurement in the United States: A Brief History and Review of Current Methods.* Proceedings of the Worldwide Readership Symposium, 1981. www.readershipresearch.org
13 Hardy, Hugh S. (1990). *The Politz Papers: science and truth in marketing research.* American Marketing Association.

14 See e.g. Joyce, Timothy (1981). *The Level of Magazine Reading*; and Schiller, Clark (1981) *A Study of Overclaiming Readership Using a Recent Reading Technique.* Proceedings of the Worldwide Readership Symposium, 1981. www.readershipresearch.org

15 I. Petric and M. Appel: *The Readership Currency: Dutch Design.* Proceedings of the Worldwide Readership Symposium, 2007. www.readershipresearch. org

16 Baim, Julian *et al.* (2007). *Measuring Specific Issue Audiences.* Proceedings of the Worldwide Readership Symposium, 2007.

17 Consterdine, Guy (1993). *What Determines Readers-Per-Copy Patterns for UK Magazines?* Proceedings of the Sixth Worldwide Readership Symposium, San Francisco.

18 Baim, Julian and Goerlich, Bruce (1995). *Circulation Changes and Audience Estimates.* Proceedings of the Seventh Worldwide Readership Symposium, Berlin.

19 E.g. Lindberg, Ingemar (1981). *Circulation and Readership Trend Analysis.* Proceedings of the First Worldwide Readership Symposium, New Orleans; Lindberg, Ingemar (1997). *Are Changes in Readership Preceding Changes in Circulation?* Proceedings of the Eighth Worldwide Readership Symposium, Vancouver; Consterdine, Guy (1993). *What Determines Readers-Per-Copy Patterns for UK Magazines?* Proceedings of the Sixth Worldwide Readership Symposium, San Francisco.

20 McDonald, Scott and McPheters, Rebecca (2003). *Audience: The Appropriate Measure of Circulation Quality.* Proceedings of the Eleventh Worldwide Readership Symposium, Cambridge.

21 Perry, Jane (1995). *Some Further Thoughts on Readership and Circulation.* Proceedings of the Seventh Worldwide Readership Symposium, Berlin.

22 Actual examples are normally given in the technical appendices of readership surveys.

23 Skrapits, Mike and Appel, Valentine (1997). *The Relationship Between Changes in Circulation and Changes in Readership.* Proceedings of the Eighth Worldwide Readership Symposium, Vancouver.

24 For a list of references see: Peeters, Stef, Debeer, Véronique and Lanckriet, Trui (1999). *Magazines Deserve Time – The Build Up of Magazine Audiences Over Time.* Proceedings of the Ninth Worldwide Readership Research Symposium, Florence.

25 Dodson, Richard (1993). *Audience Accumulation and the Link with Print Advertising Effectiveness.* Proceedings of the Sixth Worldwide Readership Symposium, San Francisco.

26 Peeters, Stefaan, Debeer, Véronique and Lanckriet, Trui (1999). *Magazines Need Time – The Build-up of Magazine Audiences Over Time.* Proceedings of the Ninth Worldwide Readership Symposium, Florence.

27 Baim, Julian, Frankel, Martin R. and Agresti, Joseph (1999). *Magazine Audience Accumulation: Development of a Measurement System and Initial Results.* Proceedings of the Ninth Worldwide Readership Research Symposium, Florence.

28 Goldstein, Larry (2003). *Audience Accumulation and Advertising Exposure in Magazines.* ESOMAR Print Audience Measurement, Los Angeles, June

2003; Consterdine, Guy (2004). *Distributing Print Exposure: A New Planning Tool.* Admap, November 2004.

29 Anuszewska, I. (2003): *How People Read Newspapers.* Proceedings of the Worldwide Readership Symposium, 2003. www.readershipresearch. org; Jansen, T. and van den Berg, V. (2001). *Breakthrough in Newspaper Research in the Netherlands.* Proceedings of the Worldwide Readership Symposium, 2001. www.readershipresearch.org; Higginbotham, J. and Cognac, Bernadette (1997). *How One Research Company Approaches Newspaper Section Readership: an Overview of Methodology and Reading Trends.* Proceedings of the Worldwide Readership Symposium, 1997. www. readershipresearch.org; Birt, Hilary (1997). *The Measurement of Newspaper Section Readership on the UK NRS.* Proceedings of the Worldwide Readership Symposium, 1997.

30 Czaia, Uwe (2003). *Pressedge. Optimising Ad Positioning in Print Media.* Proceedings of the Worldwide Readership Symposium, 2003.

31 See *The Quality of Reading Survey,* Ipsos-RSL (2000) for a full list of measures.

32 Meier, Erhard (2007). *Summary of Current Readership Research.* Proceedings of the 13th Worldwide Readership Symposium, Vienna, October 2007.

33 Ware, Britta, Baron, Roger and Edge, J. (2005). *Identifying Key Metrics for Magazine Planning.* Proceedings of the 12th Worldwide Readership Symposium, Prague, October 2005.

34 Affinity Research (2004–2006) *Fine Print* I–VII. http://www.affinityresearch. net/pages/3/index.htm

35 Smith, Alan (1999). *How Campaign Tracking Studies & Econometric Modelling Can Undervalue Advertising Benefits.* International Journal of Advertising, Vol. 18, No. 2, 1999; Brown, Gordon (1994). *The Awareness Problem,* Admap, January 1994; Smith, Alan (1997). *More Food for Thought.* Admap, February 1997.

36 Ephron, Erwin (2005). *The Softer Intrusion of Print.* Admap, June 2005.

37 For results of several studies on this see Franzen, Giep (1994). *Advertising Effectiveness.* NTC Publications.

38 The billetts Consultancy (November 2002). *New premiums & new discounts for press advertisers.*

39 http://www.ppamarketing.net/cgi-bin/wms.pl/664

40 Smit, Edith, Neijens, Peter and Sturman, Marijntje (2006). *It's all about Catching the Reader's Attention.* In *International Advertising and Communication. Current Insights and Empirical Findings.* DUV.

41 Walker, James and Cardillo, Daniele (1998). *Does Size Matter (or position, or colour, or context…)?* Admap, January 1998. Also Foley, Tim (1999). *When Late Left Beats Early Right.* Proceedings of the Ninth Worldwide Readership Symposium and Franzen (*ibid*).

42 *Everything on the Impact of Advertisements in Magazines.* Stop/watch (2005). Available from FIPP at www.fipp.com

43 http://www.magazine.org/advertising/guidelines/recall.aspx

44 Newspaper Association of America (April 2009). *Newspaper Web Site Audience Increases More Than Ten Percent In First Quarter To 73.3 Million Visitors.* http://www.naa.org/PressCenter/SearchPressReleases/2009/ Newspaper-Web-Site-Audience-Increases-More-Than-Ten-Percent.aspx

45 Magazine Publishers Association (May 2009). *Magazine Digital Initiatives Help Drive Growth to Publisher's Websites.* http://www.magazine.org/association/press/mpa_press_releases/magazine-web-traffic-digital-initiatives-q1-2009.aspx

46 Savage, M. (2008). *You Only Live Twice.* The Asia Media Journal, Q2 2008.

47 Cauthorn, R. (2006). *The New World Order of Newspaper Advertising – A Change in Direction.* International Newsmedia Marketing Association, December 2006.

Chapter 3: Measuring Out of Home audiences

1 ZenithOptimedia (14 April 2009). *Advertising Expenditure Forecasts,* April 2009.

2 Green, Andrew (2006). *Are So-called Ambient Media Just Stunts?* WARC Media FAQ, October 2006; Shankar, A. and Horton, B. (1999). *Ambient Media: advertising's new opportunity?* IJA, 1999.

3 Taylor, C. and Franke, G. (2003) *Business Perceptions of the Role of Billboards in the US Economy.* JAR Vol. 43, No. 2, June 2003.

4 http://www.postar.co.uk/market-summary (February 2009).

5 http://english.peopledaily.com.cn/200512/03/eng20051203_225407.html

6 OAAA (29 June 2009). *Outdoor Outlook.* http://www.oaaa.org

7 Shankar, Avi and Horton, Brett (1999). *Ambient Media: advertising's new opportunity?* International Journal of Advertising.

8 Bloom, Derek (1994). *The Audience to Outdoor Posters.* Chapter in Kent, Raymond (ed.) (1994) *Measuring Media Audiences.* Routledge.

9 Copland, Brian (1963). *A Review of Poster Research,* Business Publications.

10 McEvoy, David and Hoy, Rachel (2003). *50 Years of Outdoor Research.* Admap, Issue 440.

11 Philpott, Joseph, Mattlin, Jay and Walsh, Peter (2007). *More than Just a Survey: Considerations for Selecting an Integrated Approach to Audience Measurement.* ESOMAR, June 2007.

12 Kloprogge, Peter, van der Kooi, Marcel and van Meurs, Lex (2003). *The Dutch Outdoor Study.* ESOMAR, June 2003.

13 Garland, Ian and Malley, W. (2004). *Early Learnings from Chicago.* ESOMAR, June 2004; Garland, Ian and Doe, Pete (2005). *E Pluribus Unum – Lessons Learned in Creating a New Currency for the Outdoor Industry.* ESOMAR, June 2005; Pasquier, M. and Mende, F. (2005). *Modelling and Prospects for Audience Measurement of Outdoor Advertising Using GPS Devices.* ESOMAR, June 2005.

14 Bloom, Derek (2004). *Applying Professional Surveying Methods to Outdoor Visibility.* ESOMAR, June 2004; Miranda, A. (2004) *VAI Experience in Latam.* ESOMAR, June 2004.

15 Mansell, Nigel (1997). *Rating POSTAR.* Admap, September 1997.

16 Rickard, Annie (2001). *Outdoor Building Growth on Research.* Admap, Issue 423.

17 Cox, S. (2007). *Total Recall: Advertising Exposure and Engagement.* Admap, February 2007.

18 ESOMAR (7 May 2009). *Global Guidelines on Out-of-Home Audience Measurement*. http://www.esomar.org

Chapter 4: Measuring Radio Audiences

1 Milestones: Westinghouse radio station KDKA, 1920. http://www. ieeeghn.org/wiki/index.php/Milestones:Westinghouse_Radio_Station_ KDKA,_1920
2 ZenithOptimedia (14 April 2009). *Advertising Expenditure Forecasts*. http:// www.zenithoptimedia.com/gff/pdf/Adspend%20forecasts%20April%20 2009.pdf
3 Papazian, Ed (2008). *Radio Dimensions 2008*. Media Dynamics.
4 Keith, Michael C. (2007). *The Radio Station: Broadcast, Satellite and Internet*. Focal Press.
5 http://en.wikipedia.org/wiki/Radio
6 CS Ad Expenditure Dataset, v. 1.11. http://spreadsheets.google.com/ pub?key=p9LENaiKJeoyBX4eR1FZEEw
7 Kasza, Gregory J. (1988) *The State and the Mass Media in Japan 1918–1945*. University of California Press.
8 Kasza, Gregory J. (1988) *Ibid*.
9 Chappell, Matthew and Hooper, C.E. (1944) *Radio Audience Measurement*. Stephen Daye, New York.
10 Belville, Hugh Malcolm, (1985). *Audience Ratings. Radio, Television, Cable*. Lawrence Erlbaum Associates.
11 Chappell, Matthew and Hooper, C.E. (1944) *Ibid*.
12 Belville, Hugh Malcolm, (1985). *Ibid*.
13 Saal, Rene, de Saint Roman, Arnaud and Le Moal, Odile (1995). *Diary vs. Recall. Mediametrie Complementary Approaches for Measuring Radio Audiences*. ESOMAR Radio Research Symposium, July 2005.
14 Chan, David and Charlebois, Owen (1996). *A Comparison of Ratings Methods: Telephone vs. Diary*. ESOMAR Marketing & Research Today, March 1996.
15 Belville (1985). *Ibid*. pp.342–344.
16 Warsia, Noor Fathima (2007) *Diary vs. DAR radio pilot: Day-after-Recall gets the MRUC thumbs up, so far*. Exchange4Media.com 22 September 2007.
17 Meneer, Peter (1995). *Radio Audience Measurement Systems Across Europe: Currencies in Common or in Conflict?* ESOMAR Radio Research Symposium, July 1995.
18 Kennedy, Paul (2003) *And Now For Something Completely Different?* Admap, October 2003.
19 http://www.arbitron.com/international/ppmworldmap.htm
20 Webb, Beth M. and Patchen, Robert H. (2003). *A Full Year of Audience Measurement with PPM*. ESOMAR Radio Audience Measurement, Los Angeles, June 2003.
21 Vancraeynest, Dominique and Dequeldre, Philippe (2007). *Put the Radiometer On! Will a Switch to Electronic Measurement Ruin Our Currency in Belgium?* ESOMAR WM3, Dublin, June 2007.
22 E.g. www.rab.co.uk

23 Media Dynamics. (2005) *Radio Dimensions*. pp.129–142.
24 Radio Advertising Effectiveness Laboratory (2002). *Research Compendium*.
25 Bureau de Commercialisation de la Radio du Québec (1997). *Summary of Research Conducted by Descarie & Complices* (RAEL # 026).
26 Thalberg, Jarle (1999). *The Relationship Between Awareness Tracking and Media Investments*. ESOMAR (RAEL # 010).
27 Ferris, Jackie and Charlebois, Owen (1999). *A Comparison of Radio and TV Advertising Recall*. ESOMAR (RAEL # 008).
28 Galen, Robert (1987) *PreTesting Company – Comparing Radio and TV Commercials*. RAB (RAEL # 020).
29 Gould, Heather (1996) *The Ironing Board Revisited*. Admap (RAEL # 122).
30 Radio Advertising Bureau UK (1981). *The Jigsaw Study*. (RAEL # 027).
31 Radio Marketing Bureau Canada (1997). *Imagery Generation and Transfer Study*. (RAEL # 022).
32 Virgin Radio (1995). *The Mind's Eye – Can Television Advertising be Visually Transferred by the Medium of Radio?* ESOMAR (RAEL # 023).
33 Statistical Research. (1993). *Imagery Transfer: TV Pictures in the Radio Listener's Mind*. (RAEL # 123).
34 More, Roderick (January 2005) *How to Make the Most of Radio*. Admap. Also: Fitch and Herr (January 2003) *The Media Multiplier Effect*. Millward Brown Perspectives 21.
35 Harding, John and Ratcliffe, William (October 2003) *radio active*. Admap.
36 Radio Advertising Effectiveness Laboratory (2004). The Benefits of Synergy: Moving Money into Radio. http://radioadlab.com/library/rael_benefits_of_synergy.pdf
37 Wild, Christoph (June 1999). *With and Without Help Radio Campaign Work*. ESOMAR. Radio on the World Stage, Boston.
38 RAB (2006). *The Radio Multiplier Study*. http://www.rab.co.uk/rab2006/showcontent.aspx?id=466
39 Janssens, W. and De Pelsmacker, P. (2005) *Emotional or Informative? Creative or Boring? The Effectiveness of Different Types of Radio Commercial*. International Journal of Advertising Research, Vol. 24, No. 3.
40 Riebe, E. and Dawes, J. (2006) *Recall of Radio Advertising in Low and High Advertising Clutter Formats*. International Journal of Advertising, Vol. 25, No. 1.
41 Kennedy, Paul (5 November 2008). *Balance and Perspective. Establishing Priorities for UK Radio Audience Measurement for the Next 3–5 Years*. ASI Radio Conference, Lisbon.

Chapter 5: Measuring television audiences

1 ZenithOptimedia (14 April 2009). *Advertising Expenditure Forecasts*.
2 Fisher, David E. and Fisher, Marshal Jon (1996). *Tube. The Invention of Television*. Counterpoint.
3 Green, Andrew (2000). *From Mao to the Millennium: Chinese Television in Transition*. BMRB.
4 Noam, Eli (1991). *Television in Europe*. Oxford University Press.

5 Braun, Jacques and Callay, Alexandre (May 2009). *TV Consumption is Growing*. ESOMAR WM3 Conference, Stockholm.
6 Green, Andrew (2007). Chapter on Media Research in ESOMAR's *Market Research Handbook, Fifth Edition*. ESOMAR.
7 Poltrack, David (1997). *Needed: A New Paradigm for Media Evaluation by Advertisers*. ESOMAR Global Future Conference, Lisbon, July 1997.
8 Twyman, Tony (1988). *Towards a European Standard for Television Audience Measurement*. ESOMAR Media and Media Research Conference, Madrid, April 1988.
9 Kasari, Heikki J. (October 2006). *Peoplemeter Systems in the Changing TV Climate*. Admap.
10 Reubens, William (1991). *Media Research: Peoplemeters in the USA – the Promise and the Reality*. Admap, March 1991.
11 Pellegrini, Pasquale and Purdye, Ken (2004). *Passive versus Button Pushing. A Comprehensive Comparison from Parallel TV Meter Panels in Quebec*. ESOMAR Television Audience Conference, Geneva, June 2004.
12 Wilcox, Steve (2000). Sampling and Controlling a TV Audience Measurement Panel. JMRS, December; Nielsen Media Research (2007). *Television Audience 2006*; Doe, Pete (2003). *Understanding Zero Ratings*. Admap, December 2003.
13 BARB, April 2009.
14 Ephron, Erwin (1998). *The Case of the Near-Sighted Bombardier*. ESOMAR.
15 Gray, Stu and Ephron, Erwin (2001). *Why We Can't Afford to Measure Viewers*. Journal of Advertising Research, Jan/Feb.
16 http://www.marketresearchworld.net/index.php?option=content&task=view&id=1501&Itemid=
17 Harvey, Bill (June 2004). *Better Audience Measurement through the Research Integration of Set-Top Box Data*. ESOMAR TV Audience Conference, Geneva.
18 Dobinson, Julian (April 2005). *SkyView: Deeper Insights from a Set-top box Panel*. ESOMAR Conference on Panel Research, Budapest; Bristowe, Lucy (November 2006). *Sky+ – Revolution or Evolution?* MRG Conference, Vienna.
19 http://www.multichannel.com/article/279305-Cover_Story_Thinking_Inside_the_Box.php
20 http://www.reuters.com/article/technologyNews idUSTRE4BG5GH20081217
21 Statistics Finland (2008). *Telecommunications 2007*. http://www.stat.fi/til/tvie/2007/tvie_2007_2008-06-05_kat_001_en.html
22 Poltrack, David (1997) *Needed: a New Paradigm for Media Evaluation by Advertisers*. ESOMAR Global Future Conference, Lisbon.
23 For example, see Lodish, Leonard and Lubetkin, Beth (1992). *General Truths? Nine Key Findings from IRI Test Data*. Admap. February.
24 Lloyd, David W. and Clancy, Kevin J. (1991). *CPMs versus CPMIs: Implications for Media Planning*. Journal of Advertising Research.
25 Nazaroff, Annette and Byfield, Sheila (June 2003). *Purple GRPs*. ESOMAR TV Audience Measurement Conference, Los Angeles; Swallen, Jon (November 2000) *Time is on Our Side: Viewing Duration and Ad Effectiveness*. Admap.

26 Poltrack, David (July 1997). *Ibid;* Viacom explores the relative impact of advertising. http://www.thinkbox.tv/server/show/ConCaseStudy.1236

27 Zack, Barbara (February 2006). *Accounting for Engagement.* Admap.

28 Brace, Ian, Edwards, Louise and Nancarrow, Clive (2002). *I Hear You Knocking. Can Advertising Reach Everybody in the Target Audience?* International Journal of Market Research, Vol. 44, No. 2.

29 Media Dynamics. (2003). *Television Dimensions 2003.* p.152.

30 Screen Digest (2008). *DVD Sales Rise Again in 2007 Despite Market Maturity.* Screen Digest August 2008; NPD (2008). *Household Penetration Study: Ownership Landscape 2008.*

31 MediaPost (6 July 2006) *ABC Looks Beyond Upfront to DVR, Commercial Ratings Issues.* http://publications.mediapost.com/index.cfm?fuseaction=Articles.showArticleHomePage&art_aid=45264

32 IMS Research (2008). *103m EU homes to have a PVR by 2013, predicts IMS Research.* http://www.connectedtv.eu/tag/pvr/

33 Foote, Nigel (December 2005). *Fast Forward to the Future of TV.* Admap.

34 TiVo press release, 12 March 2009. http://www.tivo.com/assets/pdfs/press/TiVoARMJanuary09.pdf

35 Goode, Alistair (January 2006). *What happens at x30 fast-forward?.* Admap; Poltrack, David (December 2005). *Outlook for the Broadcast Networks.* UBS 33rd Annual Media Week Conference.

36 Siefert, Caleb, Gallent, Janet, Jacobs, Devra, Levine, Brian, Stipp, Horst and Marci, Carl (2008). *Biometric and eye-tracking insights into the efficiency of information processing of television advertising during fast-forward viewing.* International Journal of Advertising. Vol. 27, No. 3.

37 http://blog.hulu.com/2009/3/12/one-year-anniversary

38 OMD (September 2003). *Better Scheduling for Bigger Profits.* New York.

39 Network Television Association (1990). Analysis of Nielsen meter data in four cities.

40 http//www.IAGR.net

41 http://www.thinkbox.tv/index.html

42 billetts (1998) *Commercial Break Ecology.*

43 Mundy, Chris (June 2004). *Where is Broadcast Media Really Going?* Admap Media Research Conference

44 *TV Dimensions 2006* provides a summary of various recall studies, p.374 .

45 Deutsche Bank (May 2004). *Commercial Noise – Why TV Advertising does not Work for Mature Brands.*

Chapter 6: Measuring internet audiences

1 Peterson, Eric T. (30 April 2009) *What, Exactly, is a Cookie?* http://www.audiencedevelopment.com/node/2922

2 Internetworldstats.com, March 2009.

3 Point Topic (June 2009). *World Broadband Statistics: Q1 2009.*

4 IDC White Paper (March 2008). *The Diverse and Exploding Digital Universe.*

5 http://www.worldwidewebsize.com/

6 http://www.dtc.umn.edu/mints/home.php

7 Nielsen Online (March 2009). Home panels.

8   Magazine Publishers' Association (June 2009). *The Magazine Handbook 2009/10*. http://www.magazine.org
9   ZenithOptimedia (April 2009) *Advertising Expenditure Forecasts*.
10 IAB and PricewaterhouseCoopers (March 2009) *2008 Internet Advertising Revenue Report*.
11 IAB Europe (11 June 2009). *European online advertising statistics across 19 countries*. http://www.iabuk.net/en/1/iabeuropereleasesonlinead expenditureresearch110609.mxs
12 IAB (2009). *IAB Online Adspend Study*, 2008.
13 Nielsen Online (February 2008). *Trends in Online Shopping*. http://th.nielsen.com/site/documents/GlobalOnlineShoppingReportFeb08.pdf
14 Council for Research Excellence (26 March 2009). *Ground-breaking Study of Video Viewing Finds Younger Boomers Consume More Video Media Than Any Other Group*. http://www.researchexcellence.com/news/032609_vcm.php
15 Web Analytics Association (2006). *Web Analytics 'Big Three' Definitions. Version 1.0*. http://webanalyticsassociation.org/attachments/committees/5/WAA-Standards-Analytics-Definitions-Big-3-20061206.pdf; Internet Advertising Bureau (2009). Audience Reach Measurement Guidelines. http://www.iab.net/media/file/audience_reach_022009.pdf
16 www.mediaweek.com (29 September 2006)
17 Lovett, John (19 February 2009). *A Framework for Multicampaign Attribution Measurement*. Direct Marketing Professionals.
18 http://www.mediapost.com/publications/index.cfm?fa=Articles.showArticle&art_aid=28883
19 comScore press release (16 April 2007). *Cookie-Based Counting Overstates Size of Web Site Audiences*.
20 Nielsen Online (March 2009). *Monthly Newsletter*. http://www.nielsen-online.com/resources.jsp?section=newsletter_em_filter&nav=8
21 Advertising Research Foundation (April 2009). *comScore Media Metrix. US Methodology. An ARF Research Review*. http://thearf-org-aux-assets.s3.amazonaws.com/downloads/research/comScore-RReview.pdf
22 Molenaar, Rob, Verhulst, Enrico and Appel, Marion (2004). *Webmeter. Internet Audience Measurement for Media Planning*. ESOMAR.
23 http://www.hitwise.com/press-center/hitwiseHS2004/google-searches-apr-09.php
24 Quantcast (24 June 2008). *Cookie Corrected Audience Data*. http://www.quantcast.com/white-papers/quantcast-cookie-corrected-audience-white-paper.pdf
25 Pellegrini, Pasquale A. (2009). *Panel-Centric Hybrid Measurement*. ESOMAR WM3 Conference, May 2009.
26 http://www.iabuk.net/media/images/iabBrandEngagementStudy_1430.pdf
27 Online Publishers' Association (January 2009). *Improving Ad Performance Online*. http://www.online-publishers.org/media/image/Improving%20Ad%20Effectiveness%20Online_OPA_01%202009.pdf
28 Nielsen Online (April 2009) *The Global Online Media Landscape*. http://nielsen-online.com/emc/0904_report/nielsen-online-global-lanscapefinal1.pdf

29 Litton, Lesle, Nagy, Judit and Wortman, Nathan (March 2009). *Advertising on Social Networks Drives In-Store Sales.* http://thearf-org-aux-assets. s3.amazonaws.com/annual/pdf/MySpace-comScore-dunhumbyUSA.pdf
30 http://www.theregister.co.uk/2009/03/31/kuneva_behavioural/
31 Gibbon, Tim and Hawkes, Rachel (May 2009). *Get the Measure of Social Media Response.* Admap.
32 Greenstreet, Mark and Protheroe, Jonny (June 2009). *Isolating and Measuring the Brand Effect of Search Advertising.* Admap.

Chapter 7: Measuring mobile media

1 Peterson, Eric, Berger, Michiel and Pottjegort (June 2009). *The Truth About Mobile Analytics.* http://www.nedstat.com/white-paper/uk.html
2 International Telecommunication Union (2009). *Measuring the Information Society.* http://www.itu.int/ITU-D/ict/publications/idi/2009/material/IDI 2009_w5.pdf
3 Tomi Ahonen Almanac (2009). http://www.tomiahonen.com/ebook/almanac.html
4 International Telecommunication Union (2009). *Ibid.*
5 Sharma, Chetan (2009). *Global Wireless Data Market – 2008 Update.* http://www.slideshare.net/chetansharma/global-wireless-data-market-2008-update-april-2008-chetan-sharma-consulting-1355014
6 Laytner, Lance (2008). *Star Trek Tech.* Edit International. http://www.editinternational.com/read.php?id=4810edf3a83f8
7 http://communities-dominate.blogs.com/brands/2009/02/as-mobile-industry-meets-in-barcelona-3g-is-now-a-success.html
8 http://apple20.blogs.fortune.cnn.com/2009/06/10/apple-fact-check-50000-iphone-apps/
9 TNS (2009). *Global Telecoms Insights.* http://www.tnsglobal.com/news/news-1C53E642AFFB4FF79CFBF3EACA107C41.aspx
10 Frank N. Magid Associates (2009). *Magid Mobile Content Study.* http://www.magid.com/company_info/news_article.asp?articleID=3103
11 Digital Home (2009). *Study Looks at Internet Usage on Mobile Phones.* 22 May 2009. http://wwwdigitalhome.ca/content/view/3725/282/
12 comScore (March 2009). *Mobile internet becoming a daily activity for many.* http://www.comscore.com/Press_Events/Press_Releases/2009/3/Daily_Mobile_Internet_Usage_Grows
13 Nielsen (2009). *Television, Internet and Mobile Usage in the US.* http://blog.nielsen.com/nielsenwire/wp-content/uploads/2009/05/nielsen_threescreenreport_q109.pdf
14 Screen Digest (May 2009). *Strong Korean Mobile Games Scene.*
15 http://www.gartner.com/it/page.jsp?id=634928
16 Marek, Manfred (January 2009). *Measuring the Mobile Audience.* Research World.
17 http://www.mobilemarketer.com/cms/news/research/2716.html
18 Admob (April 2009). *Mobile Metrics Report.* http://metrics.admob.com/wp-content/uploads/2009/05/admob-mobile-metrics-april-09.pdf
19 GSMA (2009). *Mobile Media Metrics Study.*

20 Mobile Marketing Association (November 2008). *Mobile Measurement Ad Currency Definitions*. http://mmaglobal.com/adcurrencies.pdf

Chapter 8: Integrating media audience Measurement

1 http://www.tgisurveys.com/
2 Licastro, Giorgio (May 2009). *Single Source Multimedia Audience Measurement. The Eurisko Media Monitor*. ESOMAR WM3 conference, Stockholm, May 2009.
3 http://www.integration-imc.com/Mca-Calibration.asp

Index